THE COURAGE
TO RAISE A
Gentleman

*Building
the Foundation of
an Extraordinary Life
For Self, Family
and Humanity*

LOREN LAHAV

PROUD MOM, INTERNATIONAL SPEAKER,
LIFE AND BUSINESS COACH

Foreword by Bob Proctor

Printed in the United States of America.

First Printing: 2019

Published by Author's Publishing

ISBN: 978-1-936839-34-6

Dedication

To the future generations, may you always remember to do the right thing every day of your life; to know the little things DO matter.

My boys, Jos and Quinn, for always treating people with care and respect.

Josua aka Jos, has always been a gentleman ever since he was a little boy always going the extra mile to think of the little things that would make people feel appreciated from a hug to a card. He is all about being responsible and always is the smartest dresser!

Quinn, my creative genius who is all about independence and expressing his creativity. His hugs make me feel so safe and loved.

My baby girl, Asher. Your kindness to every living creature describes your gentle soul; how you are always thinking of ways to give back. Someone will be very lucky to be your partner one day!

My girls, Samantha and Danielle.

My dad, the ultimate gentleman, smiling down from Heaven.

My mom, Arlene, for being an awesome role model, always believing in me and always reminding me to stay true to my dreams.

My husband, Z, who reminds me that Gentlemen DO exist! He is my number one fan. He is the ultimate gentleman through his actions and his values. He is always cheering me on with every crazy idea I come up with. Who would have known baggage claim would lead to this? So grateful it did!

Acknowledgements

YOU, for picking up this book because you know being a gentleman DOES MATTER!

Jos, my eldest son who is a spitting image of my dad...the ultimate gentleman.

Quinn, my son who loves and appreciates all the beauty all around and within us.

Asher, my gorgeous daughter who is a heart with legs.

Z, my husband who is my number one Raving Fan.

Lego, Mojo and Buddy, my hairy sons who have always been elegant gentlemen.

Danielle, my future Daughter in law, a woman I love and respect with all of my heart.

My Bonus daughter Samantha who is going to be an amazing doctor and will help so many people.

My Brother David, the most committed Yogi and Rock for his family - Lila and Heidi, I love you all dearly.

My Mom, the most Badass and Beautiful woman who always speaks her truth.

Heidi, Caden and Darren Lisiten. Heidi, you are my best friend who has always believed in me.

All the gentlemen who have had a huge impact in my life – Adam Krafczek, Kevin Donahue, Phillipe Van Den Bossche, Keith Cunningham, Ed Cerna, Joseph McClendon, Bob Proctor, David Kirsch, Eric Worre, Tom Chenault, Jordan Adler, Pa Joof, Scott, Chris Dudley, Scott DeMoulin, John Brans, Sam Hawley, Alex King Dan Lier, Sam Georges, Tony Robbins (just to name a few).

Working the NAC and getting to know all of these amazing men: Daymond John, Gene McNaughton, Steve Weinreb, Micheal Burnett, Gary Vaynerchuk, Russell Brunson, Dean Graziosi.

Cheryl Cortese, The Velvet Hammer and my mentor for the past 12 years.

Magdelana, Patric C, Kathleen, Sarah C, Patricia, Andres, Claudine, Novella, Glenda ...My Team who always has my back.

Ann McIndoo for helping me turn this into a reality.

Margaret Irving "Chili" for helping with the interviews.

Patricia Castro for being a great role model for Asher.

My Vegas Friends - Dee B, Michelle R, Tanya, Dorit, Jeni H, Marcia, Suzy, Vanessa, Dallyce, Ardi, Olivia, Christina, Jules (smiling from Heaven), and many more.

My MPW friends - Marina Worre, Lisa Grossman, Deni Robinson, Whitney Husband, Tiffany Beverly Malott, Stefania La Gatto, for your elegance and grace to be strong and powerful women always supporting others.

Mary Glorfield, Terri Hart, Heather Davidoff for believing in me and my vision.

My forever friends, Chris Dudley, Jayne, Tani, Emily, Jen Steinman, Monique Walker.

To all my Badass and Beautiful attendees - Michelle P, Patty J, Stacy, Robin, Lindsey, Erin, Anne Marie, Beth, Stephanie, Brooke, Suzanne, Amanda, Karen, Keren, Joy, Mary, Maria, Carrie, Alison, Jillian, Sandy, Terra, Kim, Rachel, Allison, Elena, Jessica, Keisha, Joy, Staci, Kim B, Terri, Teri, Adrian, Patty, Miki, and more!

The Men of JP: Jay Martin, John Blair, Mick Egan, Simon Bowler, Randy, Paul Jarvis, Peter Glennie, Paulo Teixeira, Elton DuBois, Sean Hopkins, Jeff Roberti, Doug, Steven M, James, Brian, Lorien, Ant, Luke, Ryan, Austin, D'Wayne, Adam Westwick, Matt, Ben, Andres.

My JP Family, the Home Office, sidelines and YOLO International for helping millions around the world.

Wendy, Brandy, Kristy, Leeia, Manon, Kate, Kim, Danielle, Natalie, Kate, Linda, Kira, Jess, Kristine, Fe, Melanie, Amanda, Becky, Stacy, Hillary, Mary Beth, Kally, Vel, Sylvia, Franchesca, Sally, Lynda, Zoe, Nancy, Kate, Ang, Deon, Erin, Lauren, Jess , Karolina, Eliana, Franchesca, Suzanne, Mo, Brooke, Kathy and the thousands of other team around the world!

Sidelines: Mitra, Courtney, Brandy, Jamie, Robin, Karen, Karin, Moira, Pam, Gretchen, Cynthia, Jenni, Toni, Jennifer, Joy, Emma,

Emma, Katie, Carly, Olivia, Staci, Aleta, Ginger, Sandy, Ellie and so many more.

My inspirations: Oprah, Dr Shefali, Dr Sears, Reese Witherspoon, Marie Forleo, Mary Morrissey, Cynthia Kersey, Mel Robbins, Brené Brown, Simon Sinek, Iyanla Vanzant, Paulo Coelho, Gabrielle Bernstein, Esther and Jerry Hicks, Denise Lin, Ken Blanchard and so many more!

All the crew teams I have had the privilege to work with over the past 30 years!

To every teacher and every coach my kids have had that have been there to support them.

Every participant, I have ever had the chance to meet.

With love and gratitude, Loren

Table of Contents

Foreword

Over one hundred years ago, an obscure Englishman wrote, "Calmness of mind is one of the beautiful jewels of wisdom. It is the result of long and patient effort in self-control." I believe you could also say that's a quality that all gentlemen possess. They are in control of self; they're not the plaything for outside forces, conditions, and circumstances. They go through their days with a calmness of mind. Loren nailed it when she selected the title, "The Courage to Raise a Gentleman."

I believe it would be safe in saying this awesome quality never happens by accident but it the result of a good gene pool and some excellent tutoring from a very young age.

The very reason it requires courage in the raising of a gentleman becomes fairly obvious when you are aware of what is happening. You are teaching young men to do something that is done by very few. When you take a look at the number of gentlemen relative to the male population it becomes very similar to the number of successful people relative to the general population.

As Earl Nightingale one time pointed out, being successful is not natural. It if was, everyone would be successful. You have to do things daily and continue to do them until they become an automatic part of your behavior. These are things the general population rarely do. Ergo, to be a gentleman, you have to do things and do them automatically that very few men naturally do.

Men are born, gentlemen are raised. Courage is an absolute requirement in the personality of any mom, dad, or guardian who has the desire to raise a gentleman. Teaching a young boy to form the habit to do what gentlemen automatically do is not cool in today's world. Gentlemen are not cool; gentlemen are gentlemen.

Gentlemen are oriented. They treat all people with respect. They listen because they care. They're interesting because they're interested.

You're going to love this book. Loren Lahav has done an excellent job sharing necessary information required in the raising of a gentleman. Loren has done an excellent job because she's so well qualified to write about this subject. Loren is a personal development specialist. Loren worked for 30 years, planning 100s of events, leading the crew and facilitating Life Mastery events for 18 years for the Tony Robbins Companies. She has built a very successful and personal development company helping tens of thousands of people all over the world. Wherever Loren Lahav is involved, productivity increases and prosperity flourishes.

I have had the very good fortune of knowing and being friends with Loren for a little over twenty-five years. I have watched her apply the information between the covers of this book in her own son's lives, developing them into gentlemen. This lady knows what she is doing and does it extremely well.

I have always thought watching Loren work is like watching a famous ballerina perform. She operates with such calm confidence. Without question, she is a professional. This woman's accomplishments would put her at the top with the very best in the personal development industry.

Don't just read her book, study it. Over fifty years ago, my mentor taught me that no amount of reading or memorizing can make a person successful in life. It is the understanding and application of wise thoughts that counts.

I feel very honored that Loren asked me to write the foreword to such an important book.

Bob Proctor
Speaker and Bestselling author of "You Were Born Rich", and teacher featured in The Secret

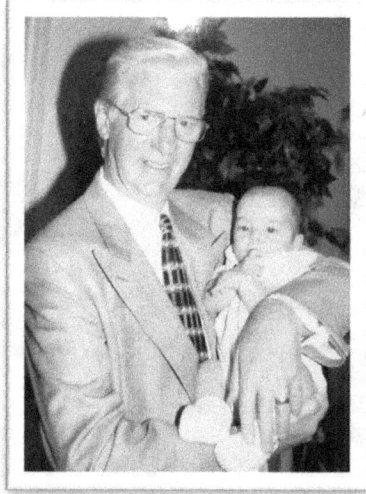

Bob Proctor has been a friend for years.
Here he is with my son Jos as a baby.

Loren and Bob

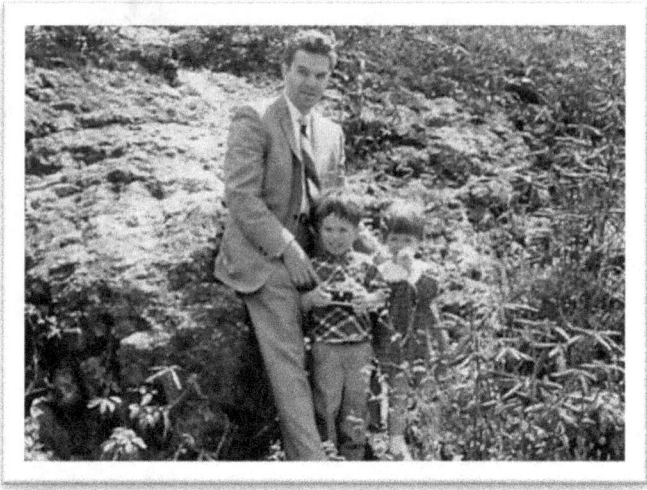

My hero, mentor, and favorite gentleman, my dad.

Introduction

As I sit here with my head spinning, affirming why it is so important to write this book, I ask myself why I didn't do it when I said I was going to over fourteen years ago after my dad passed away. I reminded myself of the words that I always say when I do talks around the world... "Sometimes, it is all about timing." Well, ding, ding, ding this truly is the case now. Just fourteen years ago, it seemed that people still said "hello" to each other, there were few smart phones, and people would actually have conversations and interaction with one other. If there was ONE outcome of this book...it would be to wake us up to have the DESIRE and commitment to have those conversations and interactions again because it feels so good to do!

June 29, 2007 came along and the whole world changed! Not just because my beautiful daughter Asher was born, but also because it was the day the iPhone was launched. Yes, I am beyond grateful for the iPhone and smartphone technology that enables us to communicate on higher and different levels, capture memories, document events and access millions of apps. If you look around, though, the cell phone has crept into every part of life ... at an airport and even at restaurants. Most people are captivated by what is on their phone, talking on them, or just mindlessly staring at them because it has become such a habitual activity. There is little or no eye contact, let alone friendly conversation (unless someone's phone dies and they can't find a charger, so they have the conversation to ask if they have a charger...sad but we know it's true) YES... I, too, I am guilty of this. The interesting thing about this is WHEN people do have the conversation, they most likely meet a friend that they might not have met.

And, this generation is not to blame. They did what they were allowed to do, and they watched us start talking on the phone, texting, not paying attention.

Sorry, not sorry, but I miss chivalry! AND this isn't just for men. This is for all of us to wake up and stay awake. Call me old-fashioned. Think back to medieval times; knights would honor their women and the women would honor their knights. I miss someone offering to lift up my carry-on luggage and place it in the airplane's overhead bin while my barely 5'2" body struggles to heft it up there. I remember once being a little over 3 months pregnant and having to ask someone if they would help me. I got the look, "why are you even asking!?" I literally felt bad for asking for help vs someone just offering to help. Not because I am not capable but rather because we honor each other when we see someone struggling. I know for me, anytime I see a parent get on a plane and they have the baby, the stroller, the bags, the toddler pulling on them…I always offer to help. Why? Why not!

I miss someone opening the door or someone helping an elderly person or offering them their seat. I'm sure some people will ask, "why does it matter?" It matters A LOT because it shows up everywhere. Doing seminars around the world for thousands of people over the past thirty years, I can tell you, "how you do anything, is how you do everything."

I have been known as a workaholic at times, but I have really been committed to setting boundaries on my time and it is one of the lessons of this book. My husband said to me years ago, "No working past 6 PM! That's it. 6 PM-7:30 PM is family time and then, it is YOU AND ME time!" I LOVE IT! One, the strength in his voice cries out: I want time with you and me, as a woman, feel loved and appreciated by my man. It also lets me know that he is present with zero tolerance for distractions or disruptions.

My husband and I literally have our "movie night" almost every night. We have been on a Denzel Washington binge and we were talking about "what is it about Denzel?" and how, in every movie, no matter what kind of movie that he is in, he has this sense of calm, strength and gentlemanly qualities – even when he plays the bad guy. No matter the scene, he owns himself and delivers with finesse. I was reading his bio; he was raised in New York, his parents were divorced when he was fourteen, he started to hang out with some kids that weren't such a good influence, so his mom took a tough stand and sent him off to military school.

Sometimes, as a parent, you have to do the right thing, even if it is the hard thing. This is one of the biggest lessons I have learned as a parent. If you really think about the qualities of being a gentleman, one is right in the 10 Commandments: Honor thy father and mother. I'm not saying that my kids and everything that I've done as a parent have been perfect; I can feel confident, however, in my conviction of setting an honorable example and teaching the lessons of the characteristics and qualities of being a gentleman.

Flash forward fourteen years and my vision has come to fruition. The time is now to have a conversation about being a gentleman. The Courage to Raise a Gentleman is from different perspectives, varying backgrounds and lifestyles, and is 100% authentic and from the heart.

The three qualities this book will really explore and in this order, are:

1. Honor

2. Respect

3. Compassion

CHAPTER ONE

Yes! Chivalry, Kindness & Values do Matter

"Tip your server. Return your shopping cart.
Pick up a piece of trash. Hold the door for the person behind you.
Let someone into your lane. Small acts can have a ripple effect.
That's how we change the world."

– Jim Carrey

Ask any man or woman you know, and he or she may tell you that a gentleman is someone who opens a door for a person, helps someone with full hands carry a bag of groceries, or knows how to treat and respect a woman or man. However, being a gentleman is something beyond the chivalry of "taking care" of a woman or man. Being a gentleman is a way of life that many high-quality men have chosen to live based on how they want to be perceived in the world.

You may say men who are true gentlemen have been raised where it is emphasized that a man's behavior reflects who he is. These men come from homes where both parents are present, where only one parent is present, or homes where a grandparent, relative, or another responsible adult raises the child OR they may have learned from a mentor at school or in daily life. I know for my boys, they learned so much from coaches that they had in sports as well as in the personal development environment that they grew up in. The environment in which a boy grows up doesn't necessarily have to be a certain kind of home. Rather, the environment should be one that is loving, caring, nurturing and calming. It is one where manners matter, where people come before things, and where a child knows and understands he is important, and he is loved and appreciated.

My father was more like a mom in a sense; he would make me breakfast, do my hair, help me with my homework; that was my dad. He had a very nurturing spirit and that's who he was at his core. Everyone always felt very safe with my dad. He made you feel that you mattered, always!

Every woman really wants to feel safe with their man. I think we are looking for a man who treats his mother in a way we wish to be treated. My dad treated his mother with respect. He would take her out on dates, take her to get her hair done, visit her as much as he could. As the youngest of five boys and one girl, my dad was always a gentleman to everyone, man, woman or child. He was even a gentleman to our animals! You may call me crazy, but it is true.

He was always respectful of who they were and what they were, no matter what they looked like, no matter where they were from. Growing up in the South, my parents always taught me, "Loren, you must understand and appreciate EVERYONE. You must be curious and get to know them and their backstory." I attended many places of worship and took the time to understand each one. There is a lot to learn from everyone. Contribution was always a foundational part of my upbringing. We would volunteer, help sell brooms with the Lions Club, plant flowers at the Botanical Gardens, whatever needed to be done, my dad would volunteer all of us! My dad was all about how he could help and serve those less fortunate. He was part of helping to create the housing authority in our city back in the 60's in North Carolina where it wasn't such a popular thing to do. My parents went through a lot together and it wasn't always easy but they always supported each other. I remember as a little girl thinking to myself, "I can't wait to meet a man like my daddy, and I can't wait to be his wife!"

I think what I learned from them is, you never know who is watching, so always be kind and not just because someone is watching but because it is the right thing to do.

My dad was a quiet, simple and elegant man. You wouldn't look at him and think "what a dude!" What made my dad so handsome inside and out was that he was so present with each person that he was with. You felt like he really gave a sh*t about you. He was never caught up in what was happening around, he was PRESENT.

The way he always treated people was beautiful, and this is not necessarily a woman or man thing, he was always treating everybody with respect. Why? Because I believe my dad understood a simple truth.

That truth being…You are either adding light to the world or you are adding darkness to the world.

Every time you say something nice, you add light, every time you say something not so nice, you add darkness.

My dad was an optometrist for fifty-two years. I remember being a little girl and seeing a big van that would show up at my dad's office with men in white pants and white jackets. The men were from a maximum-security prison. They were shackled from their hands connected to their ankles. I remember my dad treating each of those men with so much kindness as if he had a lunch date with them. He never judged anyone. Once, I asked my mom why they were there. She told me that one of the guards was a patient of my dad's and he shared that they used to line up the prisoners at the prison and retired optometrists would walk up and down the line and examine the guys. My dad went out to the prison and told them he would like to examine them at his office.

I always thought about how much courage that took on his part. He didn't care about what people thought about him seeing them, he just knew they needed care. He even thought a lot of the anger issues and frustrations the prisoners had were probably caused by having bad vision. I remember being at his office one time and this lady got so upset that those men were in the office and she said she wouldn't stay if they were there. My dad, being the gentleman that he was offered to stay later for her if she wanted to come back. He lost a lot of patients because some people thought the prisoners were beneath them, but my parents knew it was all about doing the right thing. It is about treating everyone with dignity and respect.

When my dad passed away, MDs from all over Western North Carolina came to my dad's funeral, but the sad thing was not one optometrist did. An amazing man, Dr. Bilbrey, wrote and spoke at his eulogy about how much of a gentleman he always was. It was his eulogy that inspired me to write this book.

At the funeral, the first people to show up were the men he worked with at the Housing Authority. It literally took three men to bring in the flowers from the Housing Authority. They appreciated him, even after he left this physical world.

I wanted to make sure to raise my own boys to be like my dad! I haven't always been the best mom by making home cooked meals every night or enrolling them in tons of activities, yet I've always respected them and had them understand our job is to lead a life of being an example, not a warning.

This note just popped up on my Facebook memories and it reminds me that I have focused on what matters:

Dear Mom,

Thank you for taking such good care of me all my life. For the food you give me, for the love and the things you taught me. Love you so much mom.

From Quinn

I was never super strict. For me, as a mom, I was interested in building the foundation around teaching them how to be gentlemen; I wanted them to always say thank you and open doors for others. I taught them to have respect for their elders, and while traveling with them, I think that taught them that the world certainly did not revolve around them.

I have always been big on staying current with our emotions and encouraging them to feel and process whatever it is they are going through – and there have been times when they remind me to do the same. I am very open about how important it is to just say whatever it is that you want or need, at all times.

I see way too many people who are what I call "Emotionally Constipated". They stuff and stuff all of their feeling and emotions, until one day they explode. Being current with our emotions is so important not only for our emotional health but also our physical health.

I am committed to being the hero my kids see in the world.

When I met my husband, Z, he asked me, "What do you need"? I told him, "I don't need much, but I would love flowers every Friday." Guys are pretty simple. We think they are so complicated, but they really aren't! What my husband heard was "ok, I could be her hero if I got her flowers every Friday." It could be a picture of a flower, flowers from our garden, a bouquet from the market or Costco, just some sort of flowers weekly. With that, he began to send me flowers every Friday. Yes, for the past 8 years, I have received flowers. Last week, while he was in Spain, he drew a flower in the sand and sent it to me. I loved it! What happened was, he started doing this for me and it was a win for him because it made him feel good to do this for me, and then the beautiful thing was, it also began to translate to my boys.

My son, Quinn, wanted to go to Fiji for his 16th birthday and I was taking him and a buddy of his with me on the trip. One of the connecting flights was canceled and we missed the flight taking us to Fiji. We ended up coming back to the house until the next day. The mom was all freaked out and said, "maybe it wasn't meant to be, maybe he shouldn't go!" So I was like... "Oh great, now she is going to cancel her son going and Quinn is going to be upset..." I was worried and stressed out about the whole ordeal but was able to get the flight rescheduled for the next day and was able to calm her down as well!

I remember coming home from dealing with all of this stress and Quinn had run out to get a card, flowers, Jelly Bellies, a green drink and a sweet tea waiting for me on my bed because that is what he knew would make me happy.

I remember the note said, "Momma, thank you for all the things you do for us. It's all good. Love, Quinn." I don't think that we understand how easy it is to make our kids feel like they can win. Something as simple as drawing a bath for someone will make them feel appreciated.

When you think of a gentleman, it's really simple to do little things that make a big difference in someone's day. My husband's acts of kindness and thoughtfulness toward me have helped my boys realize the importance of small things, and how easy and valuable it can be to be a gentleman.

Now my son, Josua, does these kind things for his fiancé to make her happy.

I asked Danielle, what do you love about Jos. Here is what she said. "Everything, all of him, every little inch. I love how thoughtful he is, not just towards me but his family, friends and my family. He makes everyone feel heard."

Another thing about being a gentleman is that it is much more about kind acts and showing love rather than simply signing a check for something another may want; it's about giving back and contribution; it's about actively showing up and expressing gratitude and kindness.

Being a gentleman is that. Oftentimes, we think it is mainly women who are contributors on a personal level with family and raising children. That is just NOT true. I am awe-inspired by so many men and how they are present in and mindful of all areas of their kids' lives. We sometimes forget how much men really do contribute aside from monetary contributions. I love watching friends help their children excel at sports, they join them during the learning process, men are motivated by their successes, and they believe in them and cheer them on. I remember being in Australia and seeing my friend James and his son, Tommy going out to practice footy together while the girls hung out.

It's important to have a vision of how we will show up for our kids, and men have a lot of influence when it comes to being a role model in the workplace, sports, taking care of their significant others, family, growing from adolescence into a man, and so on. We are now digital pioneers these days, and we have to learn to adapt, but the principles of being a gentleman remain the same.

Self-care also plays a big part in the foundation of building strong generations of gentlemen. It is really cool to go to the gym and see all types of people working on themselves. It is inspiring and motivating. You can't give what you don't have, which is why self-care is so important in building strong men with strong goals and determination.

There is a book called Wild at Heart, and it talks about how every man needs three things: freedom, something to fight for, and purpose. As women, as moms, it is our responsibility to honor that early on. One of my favorite memories is when Jos was about 3 years old and we went to see Tarzan the movie. He wore the whole costume (ok there wasn't much to the costume), but he had this sense of freedom and before the movie event started, he went running through the halls banging his chest and feeling so free in his body!

This is just an example of how, instinctively, boys are looking for a masculine outlet and we, as mothers, should pave the way for our boys and allow them the freedom to discover who they want to be without holding them back with regards to our own rules.

Quinn is my total explorer! He loves that sense of adventure and freedom that he has discovered through photography and rock climbing. Sure, sometimes I get a little nervous when I hear he went ice climbing, but I have to let him explore and experience life! I have to trust he will be ok. Everywhere I go, people tell me how respectful my children are. They are curious, and they are kind.

People would come to my dad's office just to see him, just for that connection; being a gentleman includes taking the time to listen and be present with others. People would tell him something was wrong with their glasses and he would pretend to adjust them and listen to whatever it was they had to talk about. They would say, "Oh, they are much better," when he never really altered their glasses to begin with. It was all about the connection he had with his patients.

A true gentleman makes you feel appreciated. It isn't how they dress or anything superficial like that, it is simply how they choose to show up in the world.

These things are in accordance with how I am raising my boys to show up in the world, the way they have learned to emulate the behavior of a gentleman and how proud I am of them, is what has inspired me to write this book.

CHAPTER TWO

What Makes a True Gentleman

"A gentleman's outer appearance may be as simple as a gentle snow, yet his personality may be as complex as an icy road."

– Jill Alexander

My father was a true gentleman. At home, at his office, on the playground, at parties and at family events, he was always a gentleman to the core.

My mom would say to my dad, "There's no way you are an optometrist. And my dad would say, "What are you talking about? Of course, I'm an optometrist." She would say, "There's no way – you treat me as if I'm Sophia Loren – you would think I'm the most beautiful woman in the world!" And he would reply, "You *are* the most beautiful woman in the world." The beauty about this was that he really, truly meant it.

This type of thinking and behavior helps women feel safe around their husbands, fathers, brothers, nephews, all the men in their life. There is freedom in being a man, but also great responsibility with how to treat those around you, and in turn, set an example for the younger generations.

One of the things that made me fall in love with my husband was when we met, he said he HAD to go visit his daughter once a month. She lived in Florida and he lives in Nevada. My husband was traveling about 18 days each month for his job so that meant he would be home just a week each month if he went to visit her. Both of us were going through our divorces and didn't have a lot of extra money but it was not an option for him not to go. No matter what!

He said it was his responsibility to go visit her, and that he wanted to make sure she knew he would always be there for her and that she knew she was his priority. He always does what he believes to be the right thing, and that is very attractive to me. Both of his parents died by the time he was twenty-one, so he had to step up and decide how he wanted to show up in the world. Now you see why I fell in love with him!

It's never too early to teach your sons how to be gentlemen; it's never too early to teach them how to give a compliment, hold the door for someone, or do acts of kindness for others. The one thing I will say, if you want them to do it…make sure YOU do it!

The Essence of Being a Gentleman: Knowing Who You Really Are
—Jeremiah Boucher

When asked in what ways he perceives himself to be a gentleman, Jeremiah Boucher shared being patient, attentive and caring. What was particularly endearing is the attribute of listening when women explain things, even when you want to solve the problem. It's important to let the process evolve as you try to understand where they're coming from. That includes not making conclusions as if you know everything about the situation. It's about sympathizing with their feelings, but at the same time, telling the truth and being direct. And honest. Giving honest feedback. Not brutally honest, but out of concern, sharing how you feel about something and how this might be good advice for them. And doing it as a friend instead of someone that's worried about themselves.

Lessons from His Parents

This insight into being a gentleman was influenced by Jeremiah's parents. His mother is a very independent soul. When he was young, he learned how to have a relationship with a woman. Those lessons included listening and learning from a woman and maybe even subconsciously picking up on how a woman feels and what they go through and learning to communicate back to them to comfort them. To support them even when you don't know what you're doing, intellectually. You just do it.

Being Grounded and Knowing Who You Are

As far as being a gentleman in today's society and culture, Jeremiah feels it's a tricky time right now. You have to *show up as who you are.* You have to know who you are and have to really, really have grounded, solid roots in yourself, because there are so many different, conflicting opinions or beliefs about what to be and what you should be in the social media and advertising world, and everything else we're inundated with. If you don't know who you are and how you want to be in your relationship with a woman, your friends or anyone, then Jeremiah feels you won't show up as your best self. In the tradition of being a gentleman, you can't be one unless *you know who you really are first.*

A Cultural Shift in Courting

From a cultural standpoint, what he found interesting is, based on talks with cousins and young girls, the perception of the younger generation is that the man doesn't pay anymore. And maybe that is old-fashioned, but Jeremiah always thought that on a date and in the initial outing, being a gentleman means the man offers to pay, and that seems to have been lost. He finds this very odd. The courting aspect is just not the same anymore. Some guys don't expect to pay at all. Sometimes they'll even ask for the girl to pay. *The full amount.* He was "fascinated" by this.

Story: Doing His Best to be a Gentleman with The Little He Had

Jeremiah shared an engaging story that ended up leading to a significant decision in his life. At a young age, he was on a date with a girl from Brazil. They were at a festival, and he had spent almost all of his money throughout the day. He literally had $12 left, which wasn't enough to buy two roasted corns. He felt embarrassed and had to hide the fact that he only had enough money to buy what he could give to her – which was only one of these corns. It was frustrating for him as a man, and he vowed never to find himself in that situation again. He gave what he could, and he had a *defining moment* where he was sick of his life and decided to never go back to that again.

But at the time, he did his best to be a gentleman with the very little he had.

Insights on Being a Gentleman Today

When it comes to offering insight to guys of any age that would make a difference, besides offering to pay and being generous when you first meet, the most important thing as a man is to *improve your communication skills* so you can actually listen and understand. What Jeremiah noticed, and it may not just be this generation, weak communication is amplified with Social Media. There's so much selfishness where you're so self-centered that you don't even understand how to really remove yourself and listen to a person without your best interests being in the forefront of your mind right away.

Being a gentleman can be as simple as just being confident in yourself, really listening to that person and helping them from their perspective instead of trying to make it all about you. Everyone wants to just hear themselves talk. It's important to listen more than we talk.

One conscious little tidbit to start with is improving your own communication through reading and writing and learning every day. People don't really take the time to write, even in their own journal. To articulate your words. Focus on things that help you improve the way you communicate with yourself. And then you can start to learn and understand how to communicate with other people.

This is the Essence of Being a Gentleman.

Jeremiah Boucher *has been involved in the Real Estate industry since 2001. Starting at the young age of twenty, he built a solid record of achievement and sales performance during his initial six years of Owner-ship & Management of a successful Real Estate Sales practice. In 2006, he transitioned into full-time Commercial Real Estate investing as well as finding or building undervalued retail business opportunities. He assisted in the creation and development of a successful Wine & Deli Convenience Market located in NW Las Vegas, House of Vino LLC. Quickly after man-agement and sales were established and stabilized at House of Vino, he began the organization of a strong team to acquire and supersede a gas station. The prosperous business is located in Western Las Vegas, and is now named, Vegas Express Mart LLC.*

Since 2006, Mr. Boucher has opened a commercial real estate acquisition & management company named Patriot Parks Management LLC, where he has been the principle investor in over thirty-two Commercial Real

Estate acquisitions over the last six years. Mr. Boucher currently owns and operates four Mobile Home Communities consisting of more than 500 Lots and continues to actively invest in Commercial Assets (specifically Mobile Home Parks & Retail Buildings throughout the United States).

CHAPTER THREE

Embodying the Essence of a Gentleman

"Everything you are can be gone in a moment,
like breath on a mirror."

– Dr. Who

A man who is considered a gentleman didn't just wake up one day being a gentleman. Rather, he became a gentleman by watching and modeling. He was taught how to treat people. Someone nourished his soul with learning right and wrong, and he understood that human existence matters more than anything. Becoming a gentleman isn't something that can happen overnight, in a week, a month, or even a year. It isn't something that a man can expect to be unless he is willing to evolve and become a gentleman. In most instances, a boy becomes a gentleman due to how he was raised.

When examining a gentleman and his ways, a gentleman isn't always labeled a gentleman. Instead, comments relating to acts of kindness may be how a gentleman can be identified. Even without specifically using the term "gentleman", it's usually quite clear that a gentleman exists, based on what others say about him when he is not around.

Throughout this book some things may sound repetitive. This is intentional. We are always running around looking for the magic formula. What we must remember is that basics are what help us build a strong and lasting foundation. You will see common truths, from the stories shared to the principles from the experts, all woven into a simple yet powerful recipe for raising a true gentleman.

- "Dave really helped out his neighbors this weekend. Their basement flooded and he just went over and started helping. He wasn't even asked to help."
- "That was so nice of Matt to open the door for that woman in the store today."
- "Chris volunteered to help that family put up their holiday lights this year. I didn't realize he did that every year with several families."
- "John and his wife looked so happy, and they just celebrated their 17th wedding anniversary."

Why don't we make these posts on social media? Showcase people doing nice things for each other. When a gentleman is mentioned in the context of a conversation, as listed above, most people would agree that what the man did for another person was noble, kind, considerate, thoughtful, and selfless. While these may be things that people mention about a gentleman, there are even more definite characteristics that are commonly found in men that define them as gentlemen.

CHARACTERISTICS COMMONLY FOUND IN GENTLEMEN

STRONG	INDEPENDENT	CARING	CONSIDERATE	LEADER
• Healthy mind • Healthy body • Healthy Habits • Healthy Relationships	• Takes care of himself • Knows when to be dependent on others	• Helps Others • Helps himself	• Enjoys helping people • Expresses empathy	• Facilitates but doesn't boss • Leads by letting others lead

Five personality characteristics of a gentleman tend to stand out among others. The boy who grows up to be a gentleman is strong, independent, caring, considerate, and he tends to be a good leader due to these qualities. Examining these characteristics further, it is evident that they are the qualities shared among all gentlemen.

Strong

When considering what it means to be strong, it's important to note that there are many ways strength can be demonstrated. A man of strength tends to be one that keeps his body healthy, yet it doesn't necessarily mean that he is a gym rat. It is truly about respect and appreciation for his body. My husband runs 5 miles EVERY day no matter where he is in the world. He says it gives him the mental strength to handle anything that happens that day.

When the body is healthy, so is the mind. We can't possibly think clearly without having a properly nourished, hydrated, healthy body. It all links together. A healthy body leads one to have a healthy mind. It's about being aware of what our body wants and needs to thrive.

Does this mean that an overweight man doesn't have the strength needed to be a gentleman? Absolutely not. The idea of physical strength through living an active and healthy lifestyle can be had at any level. I am simply stating that a gentleman with true inner strength knows and understands that being strong and physically active, either by being fit or striving to be better fit through exercise and good nutrition, has a better understanding of the overall impact of a healthy body.

Never judge a gentleman based on his physical appearance. If he's not perfectly fit, it brings up the important point that no one is perfect, not even a gentleman. However, the mindset to strive toward becoming more fit is indeed a common characteristic of true gentlemen.

Naturally, a healthy body and mind normally lead a person into developing healthy habits. This might include getting regular exercise and eating a healthy diet, as expected. It might also extend into other areas of the man's life, where he may choose to limit cigarettes, alcohol, and other unhealthy habits.

Continuing on this "highway" of health, the healthy habits mentioned here would most likely lead into the development of healthy relationships. A healthy marriage is only one type of healthy relationship, although it is probably the most important relationship in the gentleman's life. Healthy relationships can also be developed at work, at home with children and other family members, at church, and with peers, close friends, and acquaintances.

It is this overall outlook on health – which includes a healthy mind, healthy body, healthy habits, and healthy relationships – that helps a gentleman develop his inner strength. When the mind and body are healthy, healthy habits develop. When a man has developed healthy habits, he naturally develops and maintains healthy relationships.

Independent

By being comfortable being independent, a gentleman knows that he works best when he can be dependent on others. For example, an independent gentleman that knows how to take care of himself, also tends to understand the value in others, including his partner and family.

A gentleman also tends to be the man that doesn't make assumptions of other people. Rather, he is confident enough to know that he is independent of others that may be negative influences. He doesn't require approval of other individuals, nor does he seek it.

"We have a tendency to make assumptions about everything. The problem with making assumptions is that we believe they are the truth. We could swear they are real. We make assumptions about what others are doing or thinking – we take it personally – then we blame them and react by sending emotional poison with our word" (Ruiz, 1997).

Caring

Although the word "caring" tends to be reminiscent of taking care of someone, it can also mean that others are allowed to care for you. A man who is caring is also a man who knows how to lean on others when needed. In other words, a gentleman is often the man that values other people, and truly cares for others, yet is also the man that, in times of crisis, for example, knows when to rely on the people in his life that care for him.

His value in relationships is true and deep. He tends to have a good sense of who he is in life, and he knows that the relationships that he has and maintains are valuable.

A gentleman knows not to take advantage of his relationships, whether they are with a partner, his children, his extended family, his colleagues, or his friends. Knowing and understanding that life is short, a gentleman knows to appreciate every relationship that he has the privilege and honor of holding.

If you're fortunate enough to meet a gentleman, he has a clear understanding that the goodness of life can be ended in a single breath. Life is meant to be lived. *"It's meant to make you realize that you're still alive... It's a wonderful gift."* ("Life Isn't Promised So Get Busy Living").

Photo Credit: Quinn Slocum

Considerate

A gentleman who is considerate is one that understands integrity. He doesn't tend to have a desire or need for people to see that he's a good man. Rather, he takes pride in knowing that he can be considerate to others, expecting nothing in return except the good feeling he'll have because he's been kind to someone. Being there to help other people is rewarding enough to a gentleman.

> *"I started out with nothing. Luckily, I still have most of it left."*
>
> *– Jill Alexander*

The greatest reward, however, asking any man who is truly a gentleman, is the reward of knowing that he is a person of integrity, and that he just simply enjoys helping someone that could use a hand.

Leader

One of my favorite things I heard many years ago from General Norman Schwarzkopf, "Leaders lead people and, when placed in command, take charge!"

It doesn't matter what the activity is, it could be leading a business, leading a project, leading on a school board, or even leading a neighborhood watch program. Because a gentleman tends to be caring and considerate, he will often lead in the same way.

Gentlemen make good leaders because they believe in leading from the front by example, and not bossing people around. In other words, they feel that servant leadership, or allowing and trusting members of the group to lead while guiding them through the process, is what brings success to a group of people that are being led.

CHAPTER FOUR

Ladies, It's Time to Raise our Men

"In a gentle way, you can shake the world."

– *Mahatma Gandhi*

This chapter focuses on the characteristics of a strong female role model: grandmothers, friends, mothers and other female role models of gentlemen.

As mothers, we need to understand the importance of our word as being a concrete part of a boy's upbringing. This is part of your code of conduct as a mom.

One thing that I have learned is how important it is to acknowledge my boys when they do someone nice. I have done that since they were itty bitty! In this chapter I share the wisdom, stories and shares of some women and experiences that have contributed to my life and to the nectar that has contributed to raising gentlemen.

A big thing for me is that I am my word. If I say I'm going to do something, I'm going to do it. It might not always be so pretty, but at least I'm going to do it.

One day I was driving Jos and his friends to an event. Jos was about twelve years old, and he was applying for the global youth leadership program. I reminded him, "Jos, you need to call them to do your interview; you have got to do your interview today."

We are in my big suburban truck with all of his friends and I hear him on the phone doing his interview, and I hear him say, "My mom." And I thought, "Oh, sh*t!" Then he says, "Because she does what she says she's going to do." He was asked who his role model was, and he said, "My mom." Yes, I cried. It was an ugly cry.

Once again, we always think that they're too young or they're too this or they're too that, and I found myself thinking, "Wow. He gets it."

He had a friend whose dad said he was going to build a tree-house when we were living in Oregon, and his friend was really excited and talking about it with his friends.

One day, Jos told me that his friend got in a fight with another kid who kept asking him where was the tree house that his dad was supposed to build for him. It meant that much to the kid that he actually hit another student who was taunting him over not getting the tree house. Needless to say, his friend finally got a treehouse built by his father.

This is just an example of how not sticking to your word can cause harm to others in many forms, whether it be physical, emotional, or both. It is important to really do what you say you are going to do.

Most people that I know tend to feel that mother, as nurturer, is the most important role a woman can have in the life of her son. Without a doubt, nurturing a boy while he's growing and becoming a gentleman is crucial to a boy's upbringing. With nurturing, though, comes the responsibility of raising a boy, and that is to help the boy realize his own talents and potentials.

Like girls, boys can be raised with low self-esteem, which is extremely damaging to one that is working on raising a gentleman. Rath (2007) stresses that "this is why it's essential not only to discover and develop your strengths as early as possible, but also to help people around you build on their own natural talents."

When a mother is helping her son realize his potential in an area in which he enjoys and excels, whether it's in the area of athletics, academics, friendships, music and arts, or any other area of interest, her actions will help change and mold her son's ideas about the world and his own potential. After all, every human being has talents that are just waiting to be uncovered. AND when they find something, we need to encourage them to follow their dream and always show up for them.

Mothers are the ones that help their sons realize their own individuality and talents. They help their sons understand and appreciate that they are different from others, and that being different is desirable in a diverse world.

Here is what I can tell you…THEY ARE ALWAYS WATCHING! So, if a mom tells her son to tidy up his room or his toys to help around the house but then he sees her leaving her stuff around the house then he isn't going to listen to the words. He is going to mirror her actions.

It reminds me of when I brought in a lady to come organize my closets and she was throwing out tons of my stuff which I was open to because I looked up to her and her expertise. When I went to New York to visit her and asked to see her closets, they were a MESS! That was a big parenting moment for me of never asking my kids to do things that I don't do myself.

I was with my friend, Patric and asked him why he is so neat. He shared how his mom instilled in him those skills by example.

You see, when he was growing up, it was tradition within the Latin community to have the daughters help around the house and the boys go spend time with their dads doing "boy things... But his mother had had three boys and no girls. So she told them that they were all going to learn to help and be useful around the house.

She taught them simple skills like how to make their beds, separate the laundry by colors and fabrics, how to work in the kitchen, and tidy up the whole house. But the coolest thing, he said, was how she would wake up in the morning and make her own bed just the way she had showed them; before she even stepped out her bedroom to go make breakfast for her three boys!

In other words, Milly didn't just preach to her children. She raised those boys to be caring, attentive gentlemen by teaching them with her own examples.

CHARACTERISTICS OF A STRONG FEMALE ROLE MODEL

POSITIVE CHARACTERISTICS A WOMAN CAN DEMONSTRATE THROUGH HER ACTIONS	NEGATIVE COUNTERPARTS
Kind, nurturing, caring, considerate	Selfish, unkind, rude, sarcastic
Responsible with duties and respectful of others	Has no regard for other people
Independent	Dependent, needy, unworthy, poor self esteem
Loving	Indifferent, neglectful, spiteful, worrisome

As mothers we need to understand the true nature of our sons. Some boys want to go outside and play while others are happily content with a book by themselves. That doesn't mean we can't raise both of these kinds of boys to be gentleman. It's not what they do, it's who they become. As mothers, though, we need to understand the importance of our word as being a concrete part of a boy's upbringing. We are guides and set the standard for how they will treat themselves and others. My boys have always watched me write handwritten notes, send a text, say a kind word and that is what they have emulated. Sure, it takes a little bit more time, but they know the impact it has. I don't just do it for others, I have also done it and continue to do it for them so that they know that they always matter, no matter their age.

What are some of the little things you do to let people know that you care?

I love the book *The 5 Love Languages* by Gary Chapman. It helps you discover what is most important to make someone feel loved and appreciated. If you are not familiar with the book, it talks about how there are 5 primary ways we feel loved. Some are more important to us than others and they rank differently from person to person. Most of us express to others the way WE want to feel loved vs understanding the way that person actually feels loved.

The 5 are: Words of Affirmation, Deeds of Service, Physical Touch, Gifts and Quality Time. My top love language is Quality Time, but my husband's is Deeds of Service.

My boys...one is Physical Touch and one is Quality Time. My Daughter...Quality Time.

Take the time to find out what yours is and what your loved ones are as well.

I have worked with thousands of people around the world and I am always in awe when I talk to men and I would say 70% say physical touch is their number one love language.

"What is Life?
Life is a gift...accept it
Life is an adventure...dare it
Life is a mystery...unfold it
Life is a game...play it
Life is a struggle...face it
Life is beauty...praise it
Life is a puzzle...solve it
Life is opportunity...take it
Life is sorrowful...experience it
Life is a song...sing it

Life is a goal...achieve it
Life is a mission...fulfill it."
– Unknown

A friend of mine that I respect dearly, is my friend Karen Richards. I love what she shared with me.

My oldest has just flown the nest. I know for all parents this is an emotional time in their lives as we hope that the lessons that we have taught them will serve them well. Like many other recent grads, our son has gone off to college. While like all parents we worked on navigating the typical things like the FASFA, filling out applications, the ACT, etc., it is a little different for us. You see, our son has cerebral palsy as well as being on the autism spectrum.

As he grew up, there were so many challenging moments. Health issues, IEP Meetings, financial strain from medical bills, and isolation from others to name a few. Yet we knew that we wanted him to be able to live on his own and thrive in whatever career he chose. I think part of raising independent, compassionate young people in the world today is giving them equal opportunity to be successful. We made sure to put him into opportunities that weren't always easy for us to watch but were necessary in order to make him the person he is today. So we placed him in school activities like going to dances, joining clubs, playing in athletic leagues, and traveling. In some instances, he was immediately accepted, others he had to learn to navigate his own way. It is hard as a parent to watch our children hurt or not succeed in the way that we had hoped. But sometimes one of the very best things we can do is to let them learn on their own. Let them experience different emotions. Let them be challenged so that they can rise up.

He helped launch a non-profit, he enjoys running a vlog on social media, and today he lives independently: he is learning to navigate dorm life with a physical disability, maneuver through a crowded cafeteria, attend classes and become involved on a busy college campus. He is majoring in Communications and aspires to be a radio DJ someday. He is always inventing new game shows in his note pads because he is sure that one day a network will pick up one of his ideas as well. He has a special empathy when he sees hurt or injustices. People are drawn to him because we let him learn through other people's kindness and compassion for him how to be kind and compassionate to others. For us, raising a gentleman has been all about helping our son be able to create relationships. To take notice of those around him. To smile, wave, or in his case (even though we tell him some people like space) to hug everyone that he knows.

Karen, love this kid! (I will find a way to get him to meet Ellen one day! I promise!) – Loren

Four years ago, my friend Linda was producing a huge event in the Gold Coast, Australia that she wanted me to speak at. My schedule was jam packed, but she had put so much time in prepping that I felt I really needed to be there. So, in typical Loren style, I flew 24 hours to go speak at the event. Of course, I couldn't go empty handed. I had to go shopping at Tiffanys for her, get her girls some Shopkins and get her son Legos. But, if I was going to get gifts for her kids, I had to get for some of my other friends' kids! Needless to say, what should have been a carry-on bag for 1/12 day turned into 2 huge checked bags! Linda met me at the airport with this look like, "What the heck!"

I told her she knows me, I always bring gifts. Anyway, I get to Linda's house thinking I am Santa Claus, ready to open my suitcase and pass out all the gifts. As I am unzipping my suitcase about ready to be Santa, a note falls out from Jos. The front part of the card said, "I am so proud of you." The back of the card said, "Mom, thank you for all you do for us. I know it hasn't always been easy but we have always been watching and we love and appreciate you. Love, Jos."

If you wonder if I felt the pains of the coach seat 24-hour trip after that...you know the answer was heck no! My soul was on fire because my

son appreciates me and who I am. That was the exact rocket fuel I needed to deliver a powerful presentation the next day.

What is your rocket fuel?

~~

Being a Gentleman from a Woman's Eyes — Zahra Namazifard

Unequivocally, the prerequisite to being a true gentleman lies in knowing how to be a man. **Zahra Namazifard** always wanted to be with a gentleman. Growing up in Arizona, she always felt that she would have to find him on the East Coast or that he only existed in the South. Boy, was she wrong! Rather than focusing on location, she realized that today, what she was looking for was a man who is loyal, loving, committed and a servant leader, among other qualities.

It Starts with Family

Why were these qualities so important to her? Zahra grew up watching her Grandfather exhibit such qualities, which she admired. Her brothers emulated the same as they grew older and became husbands. Perhaps she attributes all the traits they picked up over the years to the classical movies they used to watch as a family.

For Zahra, first and foremost, being a gentleman has to do with how men treat their parents and their siblings. In her case, it was the way her two brothers treated her mom and their three sisters. Their Grandfather set the bar high, having been a significant role model for them growing up and she learned at a young age what type of man she wanted to, one day, marry – a gentleman.

Zahra and Her Gentleman, Babak

Zahra met Babak (*aka* Michael), and from their first date, she could see how he was a true gentleman. His acts of chivalry have continued throughout their relationship, e.g., holding the door for the people following him, or the fact that he finds ways to share his heart and be generous towards others. He strengthens her faith daily by his giving and loyal demeanor. He stays true to his principles. He shows strength through his vulnerability and his politeness.

His integrity is not swayed by life challenges and he stays true to who he is! He has a great sense of humor – exuding laughter and joy. Case in point, when she read to him what she wrote about him in this chapter, he asked: "Where is this man?! I would like to meet him!!!"

His protectiveness is another characteristic that is very endearing to her. She had never thought of the risks of walking on the outside of a sidewalk until she met Babak. He quickly let her know that she was to always walk on the inside, and he would walk alongside her, but on the outside. Punctuality is another characteristic that she admires about him, because he not only values his time but also the time of others.

A True, Selfless Gentleman

Zahra is grateful to the many men that came before Babak who showed her what a *true selfless gentleman* looks like. She has realized what differentiates a man from a gentleman and she is grateful for Babak, the fulfillment and embodiment of the gentleman of her dreams come true.

Zahra Namazifard is an AUC Detox Specialist at the Center for Stress Reduction in Tucson, Arizona. She has a BS from the University of Arizona in Psychology, an MPH (Masters of Public Health) from A.T. Stull

University in Mesa, Arizona and a MAOM (Master's Degree in Acu-
puncture and Oriental Medicine) from The Asian Institute of Medical
Studies. Zahra believes in Pioneer thinking, and as a specialist, in leading
the way. Her philanthropic work includes Project C.U.R.E. and Operation
Smile South Africa.

One of my mentors, Aleta and I were talking about our kids. She is
an amazing mom and grandma and I always love hearing her perspective on raising kids. Here is what she shared:

"You walk into the front door with your first-born son and you
look at your kids' dad and say, 'Yikes, now what?' Women today
feel like they have to have all their ducks in a row before they have
children. I ask myself, which duck would I have if I didn't have my
4 sons.

"I feel like my children are my best investments. They taught me
how to love unconditionally. They taught me to grow tough and be
tough when needed. They showed me the way to gracefully let go
of the past and go forward with integrity and hope. Some called me
'rookie mom' and grew to know that I knew the best for them all
along.

"We grow with our sons.

"It is easier to build strong children than to repair broken men."

— Frederick Douglass

"I am certainly no expert.

"Even as my background in founding an academy of learning,
doing my share of professional life coaching, I still to this day do

not know how my sons grew to be the fine men they are, with all the messiness in our family.

"My first son has become a great friend. He hauled the suitcases as a young boy to help me when we traveled. He guided his younger brothers and sisters to safety in so many ways.

"However, when he was in his last years of high school, he ran away from home and demanded several requests when he returned. He was the epitome of a strong-willed child. I told him I was worried where he was and that we were planning his funeral. What right did he have to make these demands? If he didn't like it, he would have to move out. He tried it once and couldn't find anyone to cosign on an apartment for a 17-year-old.

"Later he ended up in rehab and eventually became an incredible person who goes back to the same half-way house he lived in and brings steaks to all the residents and shares his story with them. He joined the marines eventually and when he popped off one day, he ran out of the house, and asked me where he was going to live. It dawned on me that he was prepared to defend America and why was he worried as to where he would live? Really? After I kicked him out of the house at 18.

"When I became a single parent, he took on a role that he later hauled me into therapy with, the man of the house. Note to the wise, don't do that with your young man. Here is what I recommend with these types of boys:

1. Avoid Pity Parties.

"These feed discouragement and bitterness. If you come from a broken or dysfunctional family, and whose isn't, they may blame or create excuses as to why they do certain behaviors. This habit can sabotage their success in life. Athletes, businessmen and performers realize that they need a positive mental attitude to succeed. If you have a cheerful, optimistic outlook, you'll be much more attractive to a prospective spouse. After playing professional sports for more than a decade and a half, experiencing all the temptations of fame and fortune, he met a quality woman and is now retired and raising 2 kids of his own. My eldest son has now been sober for 23 years.

"My second son did everything right. He didn't drink when he was in high school, not that I know of anyway. He was a faithful obedient son who listened and didn't have to learn the hard way. He always made good decisions and evaluated them. He saw his older brother make bad choices, so he just plain and simply didn't. You might have a young man like that, this my friend, is the reason why we have more than one child. The gift of the obedient one. The one you say, 'well heck, let's just have another.'

2. Go Where the Like-minded Women Are.

"If you want to catch a fish, you go where you think the most fish are. I always encouraged my boys to surround themselves with good values people. I also encouraged them to hang with good dads from other families if theirs wasn't around, as he traveled a lot. Surround yourself with people that will be your friends forever.

"There were a few colleges that solicited great applicants so of course this son did just that. He went to a great college and eventually met and married the love of his life. He now is successfully employed with a phenomenal job and took my place on the board of the private academic institution I founded in the 90's. He has an amazing wife and five children. Their kids read the classics, get straight A's and follow in this great man's footsteps. Those apples didn't fall far from the trees.

"My third son... You might have a son who bucks every rule and challenges every decision you make. This kid is usually the best athlete, the most creative, says he will do something and doesn't and gets in major trouble. I had to create contracts with this kid that had accountability clauses. Nothing worked. You plead, you demand, you withhold, and nothing works.

3. To Have and to Hold.

" I found myself wishing this son would find a life partner and have a marriage built upon an unconditional commitment of life-long fidelity. Hoping that this will give the two of them the confidence to give themselves unreservedly to each other... But alas, lasting marital love requires the spousal commitment to be total, exclusive and faithful. There is no way my third son would have this as his future, or so I thought.

"This poor kid did EVERYTHING WRONG. He was addicted to everything that brought him pleasure: sex, drugs and rock and roll. He was in rehab at 18 and at 24 years old. He was in jail, busted for this and that. We had a few interventions and I simply had to let go and give this kid to God. I first decided to withhold money. Then when I found out he was selling his father's stuff on eBay, I said no lunch. Of course, he didn't live with me, but he managed to find money and a decadent life of filth and disgust.

"One day his boss, his friends and family gathered around; we told him just how it was going to be. NO more of us in his life. No visiting his nieces and nephews, no coming home for Christmas!

"I sincerely believed this was the last I would see of him. I said, 'Hey buddy, give me a hug, it might be my last time I do, where are you going?' He said, 'to use'. I gave him a warm embrace and he left.

"Right then and there, I turned him over to his Higher Power, and it wasn't up to me any longer. The pain was immense, but I had a calm and a relief that I had never experienced before.

"At 4:00am the next morning, he came into my home and asked me to call his brother, my second son – the obedient one. He said that it was time, time for him to make it on his own. You see, it wasn't until I completely let go of this boy that he wanted help. After many years of school, recovery, AA meetings, NA meetings and a discerning religious life, he did find a woman who would have and hold him – my dream for him.

"I don't know if I could ever marry a former crystal meth addict, but God found a perfect mate for him. He is 14 years clean and sober today, speaks all over the US and is now is getting his master's in Clinical Psychology, while working 60 hours a week at his job and raising 3 kids with his wonderful wife.

"My fourth son – this is the hardest one to write about, because this kid got the brunt of my divorce along with his younger sister. Say what you may about divorce, but it does a number on kids. Don't kid yourself. When someone says, my spouse and I are having trouble in our marriage, and they say it's been 6 months, I tell them to come back in 6 years if it is still the same, then talk about it. The damage control with kids is ongoing.

4. To Accept What Is.

"This one is a tough one. This kid suffers from mental illness, but hey maybe not, he doesn't think so. However, this kid calls me every week, goes to church, and prays for work and lives on a park bench and has been homeless for 5 years. When he calls me, he says, 'I am just so grateful mom and today was a good day, please don't worry about me.' He doesn't do drugs but there is something not right.

"He surfs a lot and has had a lot of concussions, so I think about that.

"He won't get or accept help. All of the family has tried to help him at various points, but he simply won't get the help he needs.

This probably is the kid who is the brightest, and most talented in every area, except socially.

"The easiest thing for me to do would be to set him up in an apartment or condo and pay his living expenses. The pain every night of where is he sleeping and who is he with is at times too much to bear. As I write this, I have a large ache in my heart wondering what he is up to. He has a concrete contractor license and no longer has a vehicle nor tools, all of which he had to sell little by little just so he could eat. You see, instead of bailing him out, I feel I must let him find his own way out of this because when I am long gone, he has to know he did it himself.

"The rest of his siblings are self-sufficient and very successful!

"This kid is still finding his way at 34. I pray that one day he is well, because he is the most generous, sensitive and loving young man I have.

"In the end, we don't get a manuscript to parent. There is no foolproof way to raise young men to be gentlemen. We do the best we can, and they will do the best they can; and so it goes down through each generation. But we can make a real difference in them by how we live. They are watching us every day with their curious eyes and their wandering spirit. It is all about being the best version of ourselves we can, given our circumstances.

"I had incredible parents who raised eight amazing kids – of which I am one who stumbled through life and came out with more love and joy that I could have ever been gifted with.

"My kids are successful. But frankly, I don't care about the success of this world. I pray they have the skills to deal with the world ahead, in a culture filled with a lack of hope. I pray they share their gifts of hope, and their experiences that could maybe make a difference in the many other lives they come in contact with.

"You see, in the end, it doesn't matter if you raise a gentleman who makes millions of dollars a year or you raise another with the same principles and traditions, and he is homeless, they all have to find their own way."

A few weeks ago, I was with one of my favorite badass and beautiful girlfriends, Marina Worre. This is a woman who walks her talk in all areas of her life. I am always surrounding myself with people who are constantly growing and serving. She is CEO of Network Marketing Pro and produces live events with multiple attendees ranging from 20-20,000 people. Not only is she CEO of this company, she and her husband have a beautiful relationship and she is a kickass mom. She also has the most generous spirit.

I asked her, "Marina, why do you think it is so important for us to raise a gentleman? You are married to one of the most amazing gentlemen. So why must we be courageous not to let manners slide?" I LOVE what she shared.

She said, "Loren, as a woman, a wife and a mother who has already raised a beautiful and talented lady and has the pleasure of currently raising a gentleman of the next generation, I've found that we raise our children through trial and error. There isn't a school that I have found where you go to become an amazing parent. You either replicate the way you were brought up or, if you were unhappy with your upbringing, you try to change it so that your children have a different experience.

"The point is, we as parents are responsible for raising the next generation. So, I always say, 'Do your best, try your best, build your relationships on trust. Be truthful, be respectful, be patient, and lead by example; by being the ladies and gentlemen you want your children to emulate. Make sure the time you spend with your children is QUALITY time.' Your children don't crave all your time...they crave quality time."

My good friend Staci Zacker shared some powerful truths:

"Raising 4 boys is the best job, yet hardest job I have ever been given. I want to raise gentlemen that don't conform to the world, but boys that stand out for the world.

"I try to fill their minds with as much positivity as I can. We start our mornings with loud Christian music, then while we drive to school, I have the boys find us a good inspirational video. Our favorite is Kid President. Such great words of wisdom, that will also have you laughing. I feel by choosing how they start their, day no matter how much they fight it; I will make the biggest difference.

"Through sports we talk about how there are really only 3 things they can control. Their attitude, effort and heart. I encourage them to be the best at all 3. And remind each of them that, 'It's not what happens to you, it's about how your attitude, effort and heart were throughout the situation that truly counts.' We teach them that Zachers can do hard things no matter what. We believe there is no such thing as failing, just learning. No matter what happens to us, we get back up.

"We work with the boys on eye contact, calling people by their name, and acknowledging everyone that walks in the room, no matter how many men are left in Fortnite. I talk to them about making people feel special, and making Jesus famous. I want them to love hard, give generously, pray big, and be the best each one of them can possibly be."

As I shared, contribution has always been a huge driver for me. Quinn and I were wanting to do a "mother and son" trip.

Our styles are a bit different and I was looking for something for us to do that would really bond us.

I had bought a Service trip a few years back. I really wanted to go on a trip and wanted to go with one of my kids. Asher was too young, Jos was already out of the house so I thought this would be perfect for Quinn and me! I used all the money that I made from the I AM cards that I produced to buy the trip.

I saw there was a trip to Vietnam. I thought it would be perfect because Quinn is into photography and he could take time to go and photograph some cool sites on the days we were not working. He was jazzed! He had his shot locations mapped out and all set, got new lenses and the rest of the equipment and supplies he needed.

We got the final itinerary and originally there were 12 volunteers going on the same mission trip (meaning we would get to have some free time while we were in serving in Vietnam). When we got the final reservations, it was just Quinn and me. I asked the girl in charge of the trip what had happened and she said the other group had no other choice but to cancel. I asked her what that meant, and she said that they had already committed to fit 5,000 hearing aids and were going to be working long hours. I didn't know how to break this to Quinn...

When I mustered up the courage to tell him, he wasn't very happy. We get to the first site and learned how to fit the hearing aids. I looked over at him, feeling so bad and then... magic happened! I saw him fitting his first patient, a lady in her late 80s, he fitted her and then said in her ear, "ba, ba, ba" (to see if she could hear him), she grabbed his face with the biggest smile on hers, slipped her bracelet off her wrist and put it on his wrist. He smiled at me and worked another 8 hours straight!

That night, when we got back to our hotel, he told me that had been the best day of his life so far. Service brings purpose. I am so proud of my boy! Now he is hooked!

What are Some of the Things you can do to Bond With Your Boy?

My friend Emily Donaldson De Vito and I were talking about our kids & I loved what she shared about her son:

"As an executive and leadership coach, I have worked with many successful business professionals. One thing I have found is a pattern that is apparent in most men who I would consider highly fulfilled both professionally and personally. That pattern is really simple – they like, love and respect themselves. I want the world for my son and most importantly, I want him to have fulfillment, joy, and happiness in life – whatever he decides to do.

"When he was born, I made the conscious decision to provide parenting around emotional intelligence and meaningful communication. Those are fancy words for identifying and articulating how he was feeling, cultivating courage to ask for what he wanted/needed, and speaking his truth while saying what he meant, meaning what he was saying, and saying it without being mean. My son is a truly happy teenager and while there are moments when his confidence is a bit 'laggy', anyone who knows him is impressed with how comfortable he is in his own skin and how he actively follows and creates his own path."

Do you see the Golden Thread of all the content in this book? Raising a gentleman is OUR responsibility not merely an opportunity.

CHAPTER FIVE

Dude, Your Boys are Watching

*"The purpose of life is to be a growing,
contributing human being."*

– David McNally

Fathers and other male role models most definitely have an extremely high influence on raising a boy. Naturally, boys look to strong males in their lives differently than strong females. When they look to their mothers and other female role models, they learn through nurturing and developing an understanding of women. A gentleman can't truly be a gentleman without having a clear understanding of different types of people, including women.

According to LaRuina (2013), "the gentleman is a dying breed," and, as he so eloquently states, "it pains me to see good manners go down the toilet when you're around a lady." I have to agree with that! This is really the reason I wrote this book.

No matter how strong a woman is, it feels good to be appreciated and taken care of by the men in our lives. Call me old-fashioned but it feels good when my sons say, "Mom, you look so pretty," or "Mom, that was really cool what you did."

My dad always made an effort to tell everyone who worked in his office something nice, every day. He did it because he knew the power of making people feel their best self. Indeed, how you, the father, treat women is reflected from you onto your son. But knowing how to treat a woman is only one piece in the puzzle of how to most effectively raise a son to become a gentleman – a man whom can truly make a father proud, every single day.

There are some simple basics that society has made uncool, but they are actually some of the best traits we can instill in ourselves and in our children.

LaRuina's Nine Rules for Being a Modern Gentleman

1. Be polite at all times – Simple things like saying "please, thank you, etc.," opening a door for a woman, smiling, and showing interest are all basic manners that should be considered.

2. Don't swear (too much) – Everyone swears, we're not perfect. But swearing too much is horrible and makes you sound like an idiot, so keep it to a minimum.

3. Watch how much you drink – Can you hold your drink? If not, then don't drink or only have a few glasses when you are with a lady. Being drunk is a massive turn off for women.

4. Be the protector – Don't be overly protective like a father, but simple things like holding her waist or hand when crossing the road, walking on the outside of the sidewalk whilst she's on the inside, and take her home or at least offer so she's safe. Also, if another guy is out of line, then make sure you stand up for your girl and show him who the daddy is.

5. Be willing to help – If you see a woman carrying something heavy, then help her out and offer to carry it. Give your seat up on the bus or train when a woman is standing, show that you're a caring guy, women love this.

6. Don't talk about other girls – The worst thing you can do is talk about other girls to girls you are on a date with, it's disrespectful.

7. Be spontaneous – If you have a girlfriend, make sure you surprise her with a few small gifts or a mini weekend away somewhere. Do it out of the blue, so she doesn't know it's coming.

8. Keep yourself in shape – As part of being a modern gentleman, you want to take care of yourself. This means keeping fit, grooming yourself and dressing well. It's an overall package not just manners and politeness.

9. Be a sincere person – A gent doesn't need to lie, he's sincere with his words and actions. Make sure you project sincerity as a man.

Fathers and other male role models are different to boys. They are the men that boys look to when they decide who they want to become. There is no doubt that we are all a product of our upbringing and the environment in which we were raised. We tend to look at older individuals of the same gender as we grow up. When you take a look at yourself, maybe you can see commonalities that you share with your role model of the same gender.

LaRuina further stresses that a gentleman is a man who knows how to treat women at a level beyond chivalry. These rules don't just apply to a woman who a man is dating or to whom he is married, for example, but rather, should be applied at all times, and especially so in the presence of another woman. After all, women can be girlfriends, wives, friends, colleagues, mothers, nieces, aunts, cousins, grandmothers, and the list goes on.

The next part may seem cheesy, but it is so true! We need to think about the little things that we do that can be a total turn off.

I remember when I was writing my "ideal mate" after going through my divorce and some of the top things on my list were "he must not eat with his mouth open, talk about other women, must not bite his nails." So I had to include this part in the book. Teach them early. It is not even about other people; it is about respecting themselves.

LaRuina's Guide to Treating Women
5 Things You Should Never Do
in the Presence of a Lady

1. Never bite your nails – It shows you are bored, that you have a bad habit and your hygiene is off.

2. Never yawn without putting your hand over your mouth – Try not to yawn anyway because it's rude, but if you need to, ALWAYS put your hand over your mouth and apologize after.

3. Never chew with your mouth open – Chew your food with your mouth closed, fool! Did you never listen to your mom?

4. Never fart or belch – Save this for the bro nights. When you're with a chick, it should be less wind, more chat.

5. Never look at other women – Do you know how disrespectful it is to look at other women when you are with a girl? Stop it.

Keeley (2009) suggests that men, who are raising their sons to become reputable men – gentlemen – as adults, should follow some best practices used by single fathers who have this common goal in mind.

I feel blessed to know so many wonderful women and men from around the world. I have a great friend, D'wayne who is a single dad. I love watching him with his son. D'wayne is very clear with his son that being a gentleman is a non-negotiable! WE as parents need to set the standard. He is strong, firm and has the utmost integrity, at the same time he is also loving and caring.

I asked him what is the most important thing to raise a gentleman. He said, "Love, accountability and strength."

I love all the simple truths from these experts! It does not matter what one's religious beliefs are but having some foundation gives one strength, especially during tough times.

Keeley's Best Practices For Single Men Raising Their Sons to Become Gentlemen

- Show faith and forgiveness. All the dads interviewed agreed that their relationship with God was most important. An authentic relationship with a higher power erased their bitterness and resentment. Rob modeled this type of living faith. There were plenty of reasons for him to be bitter over his divorce, but he chose forgiveness. As James watched his father choose grace over accusing words or behaviors, James then chose the same path. Lack of forgiveness, on the other hand, can hinder any attempt to train a son to honor women. Sons will notice the dislike simmering below the surface of your heart.

Here is my input on this:

- It is important to let your child know that it's not the biggest wins, or the biggest drops that develop character. The every day steps in faith and forgiveness help forge an attitude of constant and never ending improvement.
- What do the women in your world think? Try to create teachable moments with the women in your son's life. Expose him to the respected opinions of good women.

My sidebar notes on this one:

Your ego is not your amigo little man. There are rules of engagement to being a gentleman that need to be taught.

Given the encouragement, a young boy will discover a wealth of lessons from his grandmothers, cousins, aunts, and teachers. Teaching him to learn about and respect female role models will spill over into his day-to-day encounters with others.

- Think ahead about chivalry. Encourage your son to treat any woman as he would expect his mother, sister, aunt, best female friend or role model to be treated. That kind of call to honor will spur him to action. Then, rather than leaving him confused and unsatisfied with a trail of broken hearts behind him, he will have the opportunity to reflect the heart of a true gentleman.

- Affirm a gentleman. When you notice your son going out of his way to honor or respect a woman, be sure to let him know how proud you are of his effort.

My sidebar notes on this one:

Let him know that those types of actions are what MEN do!

- Who can help? There are times when you won't know how to communicate with your son. You might see a behavior or attitude that is unsettling.

My advice:

Make sure to help find a reliable male role model or a powerful outside voice as a resource. Ask other committed parents and friends for help. Make sure they share the same values as you do.

- The basics always work. Some women today are offended if a man opens a door, but most will appreciate it. The thing to remember is to encourage your son to keep doing what is right. Be sure not to give up, and incorporate respect into other areas. Here are a few ideas that go beyond holding doors:

  o Always be as polite as possible, speaking gently and respectfully.
  o Offer to assist when a woman is lifting heavy items.
  o Never use demeaning nicknames or slang terms.

- Finally, for any single dad who wants his son to honor and respect women, model it. Ultimately, you will see the same behavior in your boy — like father, like son.

Keep in mind that this is not to say that Keeley's best practices in raising sons by single fathers is not to be applied to men who are raising their sons in a partnership. Certainly, men in a marriage or a strong relationship can also use these practices in how they raise their sons as well.

"There is a purpose for our lives far grander and more significant than perhaps we might ever have considered."

– David McNally

What men need to remember as they are raising boys is that every moment, every action, every word, every gesture, every smile, counts. Kids notice adults, and they mimic them. They mimic both good and bad behaviors of their same-gender parent. In the instance of boys, this means that they're watching men with regards to how they react to different situations, how they feel about their work, how they treat people, and how they run their lives.

Note: Children can be a great mirror as to what you are doing constantly. Don't be afraid to better yourself for your boys.

If a man is doing positive things, it follows that the boy will learn by watching that positive actions are desirable. However, the flip side is that the man who has a negative impact on his son will raise a son that lives negatively. Obviously, this is not conducive to raising a boy to become a strong, positive, forward-thinking man, otherwise called a gentleman.

"In some sense man is a microcosm of the universe; therefore, what man is, is a clue to the universe; we are enfolded in the universe."

– David Bohm

In order to be a good male role model for a boy, a man needs to have a sense of confidence and self-appreciation. According to McNally (1990), "self-appreciation leads to a healthy self-esteem, a positive self-image, and a feeling of being worthy, but it also leads to the most important result of this level of understanding: a sense of dignity, a complete and absolute respect for oneself."

> *"The most important thing that I learned growing up*
> *is that forgiveness is something that when you do it,*
> *you free yourself to move on."*
>
> *– Tyler Perry*

A common challenge that men face as they're raising their sons is that they themselves have low self-esteem, often stemming back from the time they were children. What many men don't understand is the "power of forgiveness." As McNally states, forgiveness "is now regarded by many therapists as an essential ingredient in healing not only emotional wounds, but also physical ailments [such as] high blood pressure, bad digestion, and loss of sleep, just to name a few." Additionally, forgiveness can also help a man combat "feelings of anger, resentment, and of being unfairly treated." Only by working out the problems of the past can a man successfully raise his son to become a positive man.

Here is what I have learned, by teaching gratitude early, a young boy can learn to love the failures and be grateful for the painful learning moments. A common thread in great men is that they are grateful for the opportunity not just the outcome.

This makes me think back to when Jos was 10 years old and the movie Walk the Line had been out the year before. Everyone kept saying that he looked like a little Joaquin Phoenix. My friends all kept saying, "Take him to LA to do acting!" So, I did...I was pregnant with Asher. Jos and I moved there while Quinn was home with his dad. Jos went to lots of auditions and heard lots of Nos at an early age. Yes, he got a few commercials and he also learned how to deal with the Nos which was a big gift at an early age.

"We are made wise not by the recollection of our past,
but by the responsibility of our future."

— George Bernard Shaw

As an adult, a man can learn to accept the past for what it is, and to move forward, raising his son in a more positive environment with more positive attitudes than how he was raised as a child. A man who develops this sense of self-appreciation and self-worth in himself will reflect his own attitudes on his son. McNally continues by stating that "full self-appreciation requires both a willingness to enter a mental dry dock and a commitment to remove the debris that has accumulated on the hull of your life. The debris is primarily the false beliefs and assumptions about yourself resulting from past mistakes and failures."

"Some people are making such thorough preparation for rainy
days that they aren't enjoying today's sunshine."

— David Feather

One way of looking at the situation differently might be to emphasize that a man's duty of raising a son is not a job, but rather, a journey. It is a journey which he can travel with his child as he grows. In essence, father and son are capable of growing together. A man that was raised not to be a gentleman can certainly, with this type of attitude, still raise his own son to be a gentleman. It is these thoughts of righting the wrongs of the past, by living for today through the eyes of our own sons, that can help us achieve great things as parents.

I was speaking with my husband and asked him what he learned from his dad.

He said, "He always told me that one truth as bad is it is will be better than 1000 lies...so to be honorable is above what is convenient regardless of the consequences...honor equals respect and that is more powerful than anything else for a man. Be a man even if it is uncomfortable. It is not about the easy way...it's about the real way even if it is harder...and be humble about it."

CHARACTERISTICS OF A STRONG MALE ROLE MODEL

POSITIVE CHARACTERISTICS A MAN CAN DEMONSTRATE THROUGH HIS ACTIONS	NEGATIVE COUNTERPARTS
Trustworthy; stands behind what he says; keeps his promises	Lies; cheats; dishonest to others; steals
Kind to others; treats others with respect and dignity; people matter; acts with integrity	Speaks poorly to people; selfish; mocks people when they're not looking
Loving and caring	Selfish, unthoughtful, angry, abusive
Understands his weaknesses	Feels he doesn't make mistakes; expects perfection out of others
Helpful, Kind and Generous	
Be able to say I'm Sorry	
How they treat wait staff	

It is important for a gentleman to have a clear understanding that the goodness of life can be ended in a single breath. Life is meant to be lived. It is meant to make you realize that you're still alive; it's a wonderful gift.

One person I must acknowledge for helping young men and young women understand the importance of manners is Linda Coleman. Ms. Coleman has been a 4th grade teacher for more than 30 years in Las Vegas for the Clarke County School District. Every year, she hosts an Etiquette Ball. The kids learn how to set a table, learn four dances, learn basic etiquette skills. The kids practice every day for months and then the big day arrives! The kids get all dressed up, the boys in Tuxedos and the girls in formal dresses, the limo picks the kids up, takes them to the Bellagio where the parents are seated in the ballroom. Our seats have nameplates and formal menus.

The girls stand on the left side of the stage and the boys on the right. The music plays and they meet in the middle where the girl does a curtsy, the boy hands her a rose and off they go to their seats. At the table there are no cell phones; we are all fully present and in the moment. The head maitre'd comes around and asks the kids etiquette questions. (most adults don't even know the answers!) Thank goodness I know the answers because my mom and dad sent me to Etiquette School!

Then the music comes on again...and on the dance floor they go, first it is the foxtrot, then box step and a few other dances.

It is truly one of the most special days. Would love to see how we could teach this around the world. AND...the kids LOVE IT!!! They want to learn these things.

Ms. Coleman has made this a priority for the last 30 years. We as parents need to make this a priority for the first 18 years.

I am committed to making sure that we are the change. For me, things like opening a car door, offering a seat in a crowded area – simple things that would be considered old-fashioned, but still very meaningful are all signs of a gentleman.

A long-time friend, Kevin Donahue, who I consider a true gentleman, and why I am including his outlook in this book. Here is what he shared with me on a variety of topics:

In what ways do you perceive yourself as being a gentleman?

"First things first, I honor others. This starts in my personal life. I honor my fiancé by *always* opening the car door and other doors for her. My commitment is that she never touches the handle of the passenger side door. I don't just do this for her... I do this for me, to remind myself of the kind of man I am committed to being.

"I honor others by respecting who they hold themselves to be, but more than that, I honor them by treating them bigger than they even see themselves. Treating everyone with respect and kindness makes me a better man. I always encourage other young men to be this way. It takes practice at first, but soon it becomes a way of being; a way you walk through the world. It creates confidence, clarity, joy and love for all."

Was there someone in your life who influenced you along the way?

"I'm fortunate that my father has been there for me all along. There was never a night when he wasn't at home. He set the example of what it means to be a man. He was always a protector, a leader, a provider, a solid foundation to our family. He took us to Mass every Sunday, he coached us in basketball, soccer, and was there for the other sports as well.

"He was a community volunteer and a loyal employee. Also, my Grandfather Goins became a big hero for me. He grew up poor in the foothills of Tennessee during the depression. He went off to Europe to fight in WWII serving with the 463rd Anti-Aircraft division in Patton's 3rd Army, shooting down Nazi Luftwaffe planes at nineteen years old in France.

"But it wasn't just his military service that made him my hero… he built every house he ever lived in, was a beekeeper, a Christmas tree farmer, a home builder, a servant, a faithful Christian and a good man to all. He took us camping and blueberry picking and taught us how to whittle sticks with a pocket knife. He took good care of his family until the day that he passed. I've been blessed to have amazing men in my life."

In what ways did they influence you?

"Influence among men is a subtle force. I was influenced by my father because he was always there. He was always a strong force in any moment... a silent hero. I didn't realize how much he rubbed off on me until later in life. He gave me my faith in God, he instilled in me the value of family and doing the right thing. He was always sober, I can't remember alcohol ever being in our home, and he was faithful to his wife and family.

"My grandfather showed me how to be tough and also how to do the right thing, not by telling me what to do, but by always doing the right thing. He also taught me what true love is through his sixty-two-year marriage to my Granny Rose. Papa was tough and fair and always playful and funny."

How did you influence yourself?

"As a young man I would observe other men and I would choose the qualities in the men that I liked. I knew I wanted to be strong and I grew up a skinny little guy. I couldn't even do one pull-up in the school fitness program. Instead of being embarrassed, I just influenced myself to become stronger.

"I did push-ups every day and found a beam under my parents' deck to do pull-ups on! So, I worked at it like Rocky Balboa... this skinny little guy became strong. I watched others around me and read books and just stuck with the program until this very day.

"I took my health and physique into my own hands! I have also always enjoyed working and earning money. I would volunteer to help the local paper boy until he was ready to give up his route. I would promptly step in and take over. By the time I was fourteen, I had a monopoly on the paper routes in my neighborhood. Washington Post in the morning, Potomac News in the afternoon. It taught me to work hard and do a good job. I soon was doing other jobs like mowing lawns and babysitting so I could earn more to buy the things I wanted!"

Why do you feel your health and work ethic is important?

"This was important because it taught me two things:

1. Set goals for the things you want in your life;

2. Persistence pays off!

"By the time I was in my late teens, I saw the dramatic impact working out had on my physique and self-confidence; I was proud of what I created through vision, my hard work, and persistence. I also watched my bank account grow through my hustle, which helped to pay for college and vehicle expenses, and of course, gave me money to take a gal out on a date!"

What do you think about this concept of being a gentleman in today's society and culture?

"Being a gentleman will always work, no matter which era, or the culture. For me it boils down to a phrase that I love, "Always do the right thing." Five simple words that work in every situation for long-term success. There are no shortcuts and a true gentleman knows this. So regardless of what is En-Vogue or what the culture is saying, it's important that men always do the right thing. When they do, everyone wins!"

In what ways could this be improved?

"Men are in need of mentors, but it doesn't always have to be someone in your life. I have studied men in history who have made a lasting impact so we can also look backwards for influence.

"Martin Luther King Jr, Gandhi, Jesus of Nazareth, Abraham Lincoln, Teddy Roosevelt, St. Paul the Apostle, and one of my personal favorites, Booker T. Washington all have amazing stories of courage, passion, inspiration and transformation. There are many others throughout history who should be studied as well to gain some insights and qualities that are worth acquiring."

What ideas do you have for starting a movement to create more gentlemen in this world?

"First is to lead by example. Living an extraordinary life and inviting others along the way is always a great idea. I also think that living a life of service is a powerful reminder of the abundance most of us have and creates empathy in our lives. I have led powerful service retreats to some of the poorest areas of Central America for years, which are always transformational for the men and women who attend.

"But I also believe that men need mentors. Young men should have the courage to take other men they admire to lunch or coffee and put themselves in the presence of people they know to be great.

"I think it's important for men to be on a team, whether that be a sports team, a Bible study, or a volunteer team, men need to be a part of a team in life. Isolation is never healthy for a good man. To start a movement, I would like to see men participating in deep discussions, maybe a book club where they read an autobiography of a great man; that could certainly make an impact in the world."

If there is one thing that you would suggest to start, what would that one, conscious thing be?

"As I mentioned above, it's important for men to participate in a group or a team on a project that is bigger than themselves. This is when men do great things, when they are playing a role in a purpose that can make a change in their community and in the world.

"While we are individuals, we do not operate independently of others; we are all interconnected in some way. That's how the world works! So, getting involved in community projects or a club with purpose or some competitive endeavor will bring the best out of any man.

"We were designed to be in a community and being around other good men and finding a powerful role for ourselves will generate confidence and lead to greatness. Even in small endeavors, these experiences will serve as the building blocks to create an extraordinary gentleman!"

My deepest thanks to Kevin for sharing, and especially for being such a great example of being a gentleman and having such an impact on women, whether they realize it or not.

Photo Credit: Quinn Slocum

The greatest reward, however, when asking any man who is truly a gentleman is knowing that he is a person of integrity and holds himself up to those standards. Just like many great men in history – Martin Luther King, Gandhi – these were selfless men who served a greater purpose, who had something to fight for.

It was either to liberate people or take a stand against something their moral integrity didn't believe to be right. They had the courage to access that warrior part of themselves as well as the lover, the magician, and the sovereign within, known as the four Archetypes. They had access to all of these Archetypes in order to follow through with their mission.

I think a lot of people get stuck on just one of these archetypes rather than learning to integrate them and find a harmonious balance, as the real leaders actually learn to do.

The 4 Archetypes by Jos Slocum

"I've been blessed to be raised by such an amazing mother and to be around so many amazing role models, both male and female. However, I feel there is something special about understanding the archetypes of what it means for a man to be a gentleman. I've been studying these things for a while and I've noticed patterns in what both genders of role models say they want and the reality of what is truly needed, deep down.

"For example, a book I would recommend that outlines this is, 'King, Warrior, Magician, Lover'. It encapsulates the good, the strong, and the weak side of each of these archetypes while giving examples of what they look like at their fullest. This is important for me because it reminds me that I am all of these; they've always been inside me and always will be.

"Some I wasn't tapping into as much as I felt the need to inside, and some were immature versions. Realizing this, I felt a sense of peace in knowing that I can tap into my magician when I'm creative or learning, while still keeping my warrior mindset for when I need to have that hunger for victory.

"I can be a King of my own personal kingdom, while still being a lover to all people unconditionally even if they are outside of my 'realm.' I can be all these things, and most of the role models in my life were extraordinary examples of, at least, one if not all of them.

"The most valuable lesson I got from my study of this topic is that knowing how to tap into these different archetypes is what a gentleman truly is. They all lean on each other like a pyramid; they support a fully-grown man or gentleman in this case.

"The sun revolves around each side of this metaphoric pyramid, shining its light at different times of day. Maybe it rains one day, the clouds getting in the way, and it's hard to see the light shining on one, two or all four sides at times! But remembering that, just because the sun may be shining more on one side one day or not at all the other, the pyramid of me, the man at his fullest, is still there and always will be.

"From my experience with helping raise my siblings and other young men who are in my 'realm', I noticed that sometimes the masculine mind takes over the focus of a young gentleman. They get single-minded focus on 'I WANT TO BE A _____' – insert any standard young-boy's dream here (fireman, soldier, actor, etc...), and they don't consciously think about the other sides of their pyramid.

"This is why I believe guidance from an outside figure is so important; to remind the young gentlemen that they are becoming the kings of their own realms. On this point, I also believe that it's important for everyone's 'WILD MAN' to come out to play.

"The unpredictable, fun and unchained part of the man that I can only really describe as a group of seven-year-olds at summer camp; in a place where they have the freedom to just be; the place where the rules are understood, but there is freedom to let loose and choose.

"There's no science to it. That is what I've seen. A gentleman doesn't have to be perfectly polished all the time, with a tuxedo on, sipping a martini while smooth-talking the entire party. From my point of view, it's about values. It's not about doing steps one, two and three and 'poof', you've got a gentleman. I believe that in your journey of raising a gentleman, you're able to guide the young boy by showing him what courage looks like, feels like and what it really means.

cour·age
/ˈkərij/
noun
1. The ability to do something that frightens one.
"She called on all her courage to face the ordeal."
2. Strength in the face of pain or grief.
"He fought his illness with great courage."

"Have the ability to hold on to your own values, while allowing the young gentleman to have the freedom to be courageous themselves.

CHAPTER SIX

The World Needs More Gentlemen

"...find what brings meaning to your life and make that your focus every day."

– Warren Buffett

Gentlemen are important because:

- They treat people the way people deserve to be treated.
- They have strong ethical and moral values.
- They are our future leaders.

A true gentleman brings calmness to things, and a true gentleman sees both sides of the story. With this comes a strong sense of compassion, but also, strength and certainty. I believe that being a true gentleman helps strengthen a man's clear vision of the future; he's prepared, he's made it a priority; he can not only enjoy the present, but he is also prepared for the future. That is a wonderful piece of humanity, and it inspires and motivates our young people.

I have seen an instance where a little boy misbehaved and the father was kind to the little boy, but when his little girl misbehaved just the same, she was punished and he screamed at her and she was shaking. And, I have seen the opposite as well. Those kinds of actions from a father figure can translate into that little girl learning not to trust men in the future; that behavior can easily turn into trauma that will need healing. Being in the personal development world for over 30 years, I can't even begin to tell you how much "old stuff" and trauma comes up for people!

If that little girl sees her father act like this, how is she going to feel toward her future husband and other men? This behavior plants bad seeds. Being a gentleman is a great responsibility. Not only does it make a woman feel good, it makes a man feel good, if only all men would realize that. Being a gentleman actually has just as much power as being inconsiderate, if not even more.

If a man is acting irrationally or disrespectful, we also have to be mindful or empathetic that we don't understand how he was raised or what he is going through. With that being said, if a man is a true gentleman, we must appreciate that for what it is.

I don't just have these expectations for my husband or children, it goes both ways. People must understand this as well. You can't just expect others to live up to your expectations without you being able to live up to your own expectations. Same with rules, your rules for how you want others to behave, you must apply those same standards to yourself.

I hope this realization becomes clear for future generations. It's important for gentlemen of this era to pass the tradition on down to the next generation. My husband gives me flowers, and my boys watch and now know that makes me happy, and they will do the same for me and other important women in their lives.

Be an example for the younger generations and be someone they can look up to and learn from, so they will follow in your footsteps; we have to be conscious of this as parents, as well as teaching them the importance of implementing these things into their lives. Just as it's common to pass down a handkerchief to the next generation, manners, respect, and gentleness will be passed down as well if we can set that example.

It's like a man ordering for a woman; it isn't that we are not capable, it's a polite and caring thing for a man to do. A lot of women may argue that they are perfectly capable of ordering for themselves, but a gentleman is only trying to take care of you and keep you safe. I appreciate those women and their perspective, but I also honor the traditional ways and good intention of a true gentleman.

Being a Gentleman is About Stepping Up and Being Brave Enough to Do it
An Interview with Joseph McClendon III

When **Joseph McClendon III** was asked what he thought were qualities of a gentleman, three of his distinctions easily come to mind:

1. First is **common courtesy.** Treat people how you would want them to treat you. Whether male or female, we appreciate someone with compassion who treats you kindly, with common courtesy. That could be saying "Please" and "Thank you." These are acknowledgements that may seem simple, but not as common these days as you may think. Common courtesy is something that the older generation learned and practiced, something that is not so prevalent today.

2. Second would be **compassion for other people**. The antithesis of a gentleman is somebody who has no compassion and is perhaps a bit of a psychopath. What does that mean? They're self-centered with a lack of compassion for what other people feel and think, and don't give other people consideration.

3. Third, a gentleman is somebody who is **chivalrous**. What's interesting these days is Joseph sometimes second guesses himself because in this day and age of alternatives, Joseph has been criticized a bit because he will open a door for a

lady or give a gift. But he's found across the board, a gentleman is somebody that wants and is willing to do that. It's just part of their nature.

Learning to be a Gentleman from His Parents

These are characteristics that Joseph learned from his parents. His Father was the quintessential gentleman who embodied all the qualities Joseph has identified. He was the epitome of **common courtesy**. They all had to say, *"Please"* and *"Thank you."* And open a door for a woman and let the ladies go first. His Father instilled the belief that it's better to care about other people. And he was very strict about never, ever treating somebody any other way than how you would want to be treated yourself. Joseph's Mom didn't expect that type of chivalry, but graciously accepted and appreciated it.

It's no wonder that Joseph himself is an iconic gentleman, after having learned and cultivated these qualities and characteristics from the two people who had such an essential impact on his life. He also modeled others he looked up to.

Joseph's Boycott of Television

Joseph shared a compelling story about his decision to stop watching television at the young age of nine years old. He didn't like what TV was portraying at the time, which was the '60s. For one, he didn't see any Black people on television, or if there was a time he *would* see a black person portrayed, they were always cast in subservient or foolish roles. Even documentaries about the future featuring flying cars, dishwashers and color television did not have any Black people in their cast. He remembers saying, "Well, this doesn't feel good." So, he stopped watching television.

The other impression he had about television at that time was, it was the days of Westerns and John Wayne and the tough guy character. There would be a big strong guy and there would be a woman who was crying and hysterical. And the lead man would slap her... over and over again. Joseph was raised that you never hit *anybody*, let alone a woman. He remembers seeing that, and he certainly didn't approve of it. So he shut it down. He didn't watch television again until he was fifteen.

Being a Gentleman in Today's Society

Flash forward to today, Joseph feels that being a gentleman in today's society does exist – but almost in a vacuum. What he means is that young men today are trying to find their way in this world of being equal. He believes that men are equal with women in some ways, but not equal in others. For example, a man can never have a child. Period. A man can never understand what that feeling is like. Conversely, a woman can never have some of the experiences that a man can.

So, looking at the world today, there is a thin line between equality and feminism, and being macho and those types of characteristics. But it is blurred.

Young men don't have the types of role models on either side of femininity and masculinity. If a man is too gentle, he is considered soft and too feminine and maybe even gay. If a woman is too masculine, she's considered a lesbian or a feminist. And so, Joseph almost feels sorry for young people these days because they don't have clear role models; or any examples of the real deal.

A Societal Movement Towards Becoming a Gentleman

When asked about starting a movement to promote being a gentleman, he feels the place to start is Social Media and any kind of screen, such as video and television. Start showing examples. This is about being a gentleman, but an important element and another conversation, is for a woman to be a woman. Someone who accepts and embraces the chivalrous moments without judgement when a young man is being a gentleman.

Joseph has a bit of empathy for young men these days because it must be so difficult to approach a woman and not know if they are stepping over a boundary. Joseph knows the difference. You don't force yourself. In Joseph's youth, a first kiss on a date brought with it the fear of rejection. Today, there is the risk of an unwanted kiss being deemed sexual assault. That's terrifying. If a young man extends common courtesy, this should eliminate any blurred lines or doubt about being improper or inappropriate.

The answer is to provide poignant examples in the media that impacts us the most, such as television and Social Media. Provide real life examples of a true gentleman. A real *modern-day gentleman*.

Being the eternal optimist, Joseph believes this will change. "We're going through a tumultuous time with sexuality these days." He feels it will find its center at some point. A movement that includes examples of people stepping up and being that example. Being brave enough to step up and say, "You know what, I'm going to open doors for women. I'm going to send flowers. I'm going to do this because it's what I want to do and it's the *right* thing to do." And for women to say, "You know, I like that. I love that. I want that."

It's not about surrender on either side. It's about **stepping up and being brave enough to do it.**

Joseph McClendon III is one of the most sought-after Ultimate Performance Specialists in the industry. He holds several certifications in the neuroscience arena. He taught at the University of California Los Angeles (UCLA) for seven years and is frequently called upon to lecture at other higher learning institutions such as Harvard University, and many

Fortune 500 companies in the United States as well as across Europe and Australia.

Joseph has delivered hundreds of workshops, coaching sessions, keynote addresses, seminars and training programs, as well as one-on-one therapeutic interventions. He has presented to well over three million people around the globe.

In 1986, Joseph met and teamed up with best-selling author and speaker Anthony Robbins. After mastering his teachings, he went on to design a dynamic line of human change technology products and services. He has authored several best-selling books including two co-authorships with Anthony Robbins and has shared the stage with him for the last two decades.

As a driven philanthropist and humanist, Joseph's most recent project is the development of a program with Forest Whitaker and the United Nations to foster a psychology shift in child soldiers and forgotten battle babies of war-torn countries around the world.

Someone who exemplifies the gentleman's qualities is Dwayne Johnson, The Rock. He truly is a gentle giant. There are very few people I would LOVE to meet, and Dwayne Johnson is one of those people. Why? He epitomizes the modern blending of the Gentle & Man. Just his stature alone is very masculine, but you also always see his gentle side on his Instagram posts and in how he is in the world. Anyone can tell that he is all heart.

He respects his body and is up most days by 4 am to exercise.

He is so humble and respectful for where he has come from and what he now has in his life. His heart for supporting the prisoners and serving his former university is inspiring.

Dwayne is a stylish man, he is always dressed well and appropriately, you can see he takes care and pride in the clothes he wears in the same way as he does in his physical appearance.

He is known for stopping and signing autographs and taking photos with his fans. He is loyal to those he cares about and looks after his family and friends.

I found this *Rolling Stone* interview with Dwayne that is real and raw.

The Characters He Plays Tend to Have a Few Things in Common.

"There has to be some flawed element," Johnson says. "The veneer is 'I've got my sh*t together,' but he f'd up at some point and he's got something to overcome. Then there's a down point, like in every script – but at this down point, there's a galvanization that happens around this particular character – having hope, having faith, things are gonna get better, and come on, let's do this! Generally, there's something people globally can relate to, a little bit of fun, little bit of drama, a little bit of getting your ass kicked and coming back. And finally – it's an overused word, but I mean it when I say – it's gotta have heart. You *gotta* have heart, man; you gotta have soul. The character has to be a decent human being."

He Really *is* a Super Nice Guy.

"When the sound guy's son comes to set to visit, Dwayne notices that and will make time for him," says director Rawson Marshall Thurber (*Central Intelligence*, the upcoming movie *Skyscraper*). "And it's not a social media thing – I saw so many times where he would bring young kids or kids with disabilities to set and never post about it. He just did it because he's that kind of guy."

"Every single movie, we do these events for the Make-a-Wish Foundation," says producer Flynn. "When you're shooting a $140 million movie, every day is super valuable – but Dwayne will spend the whole day with these kids. On *Skyscraper* he was like, 'Let's make it Willy Wonka. I want these kids to live out their greatest dreams with me.' So, we went and got hundreds of pounds of candy; our friends at Microsoft setup Xboxes for Dwayne and the kids to play; we had the five fastest race cars in the world, Lamborghinis and Ferraris, and Dwayne took them each on a drive around the neighborhood. At the end of the day he gave this speech where he said, 'I just want to tell you how brave you kids are. I'm blown away by your strength, and I wish I had half of it.' You're just like, 'Who *is* this guy?' They'll never forget that for the rest of their lives.

No Matter What, He'll be Happy.

"What's the alternative?" Johnson says. "To be an asshole? Life's too good. If back when I was 13 and didn't have shit, you showed up like, 'Hey man, we're gonna do an interview years from now, you're gonna be an actor in Hollywood and be famous,' I would have fucking cried and just had the biggest smile on my face. And then if you'd said, 'But the caveat is, when you get there, you have to be one thing.' I'd be like, 'Oh my God, dude, I gotta sell my soul, right? Tell me, what do I gotta be?' And you'd said, ``You just gotta be happy'?" Johnson laughs. "Sh*t – where do I sign up?"

What I love about this is the respect that he has for everyone he meets.

It is important for the gentlemen of this era to pass the tradition on down to the next generation.

CHAPTER SEVEN

Having the Courage to Raise a Gentleman

"The past gives us experience and makes us wiser so that we can create a beautiful and bright future."

– Debasish Mridha

Author Sara Eberle of Care.com provides a suggestion of ten well-researched tips, with backing from four experts in the field of etiquette, that can help parents have the courage to raise their sons to become a gentlemen. Her focus is on raising a son with "manners, kindness, responsibility, and empathy – all positive traits that lead to gentleman-like behavior and (bonus!) a giant confidence boost to your boy."

Ten Tips to Raising a Gentleman

How to Develop Good Manners, Empathy, Responsibility and Kindness in Boys
By Sara Eberle

1. Examine Your Expectations

"Know what to expect by age and personality," says etiquette expert Cindy Post Senning, Ed.D., the great granddaughter of renowned manners maven Emily Post and director of The Emily Post Institute. At each step of his growing life, your son should learn a little more about manners, such as saying, "Please" and "Thank you" from ages one to three and helping to clear the table by age five.

"Three-year olds can't look someone in the eye [see tip #4], but by six years old, they should be able to do that," says Senning, whose website, TheGiftofGoodManners.com, provides etiquette guidelines from birth until eighteen years old.

You will want to consider your son's personality when setting your goals. Tweak lessons based on whether he is shy, quiet, outgoing, talkative or inquisitive, according to Senning. "Don't pressure kids," says Senning. "Be sensitive to your son's personality at every developmental stage."

2. Encourage Empathy

Compassion is an essential trait for building self-respect and respect for others. "Kids who are gentlemen don't bully and are less likely to be bullied," says Senning. "A gentleman is also someone who stands up for his friends."

Work on perspective taking, the skill of considering another's view before your own. First, ask your son how he feels, then ask him what he thinks the other person is feeling. "This is an important stage that is often missed," says Maia Szalavitz, co-author of "Born for Love: Why Empathy is Essential and Endangered." "It's like putting on your own oxygen mask first and then you can help others." Practice by reading together and asking, "What do you think the rabbit in the book is feeling?" Engaging your son in the rabbit's view gets him in the habit of thinking of others.

3. Be All Ears

Listening to peers is essential to making and keeping friends – at all ages and stages of life. "Teach boys to make an effort to listen, because other people's thoughts really do matter," says Katy Shamitz, director of Skills for Living, a center in Norwell, Mass., where kids learn about socializing. "For the past ten years there's been a culture of celebrating yourself. Learning that it's not all about you is a dying art. Kids show caring by lending an ear."

4. Make Eye Contact and Smile!

"Remind your son to walk into a room, smile and connect with kids with his eyes," says Shamitz. This also allows him to notice how others might be feeling. "If there's a kid sitting by himself, tell your son to go talk to him. Encourage your son to use social thinking skills to figure out how other people are feeling." Explain the value of smiling, especially if he's shy; smiles cheer up a room; smiles make everything easier; and smiles boost moods.

Eye contact expresses sincerity and honesty and fosters bonding between two people. It also helps build self-confidence. However, "It could be really threatening to look someone in the eye," says Senning. "Teach kids to look at the nose. You can't tell and it's not as scary." Most boys giggle when you suggest looking at someone's nose, so it's a great way to break the ice and teach a critical social skill to last a lifetime.

5. Multi-touch Messages

"Boys often respond less to words alone than girls," says Michael Gurian, a family therapist and author of *The Wonder of Boys*. When teaching gentleman-like behaviors, communicate with three senses (sight, touch, sound) to get your message across. For example, if your son always tosses his shoes into the family room, try this multi-sensory method:

- Get down at his level and look him in the eye.
- Gently hold both shoulders.
- Say, "I want you to place your shoes in the mudroom."

Use this technique anywhere – at a friend's house, restaurant, grocery store – to reinforce and repeat etiquette lessons.

6. Act Now

Little kids forget requests to act responsibly within seconds, according to Gurian. "It's important to have them do tasks right away and then reward them with nice words. Plus, the memory center in boys develops later than girls, so your notion of how responsibility is handled should be different," he explains. When you ask your son to move his trucks out of the living room, for example, have him do it right away so the memory of the request matches the action. Or, do it together to model how to take care of your belongings and explain out loud why you put toys away at the end of the day.

7. Practice at Home

Practice table manners and chivalry at home, such as complimenting the cook, burping quietly with your mouth closed, and writing thank you notes so your son knows what to do when he is on his own. "Teaching your boy to be a gentleman gives him the skills to build and strengthen relationships with family, teachers, and friends, and helps him in day-to-day life," says Senning. "This develops self- confidence because your son will go into all situations, from eating at a friend's house to going on a job interview (later in life), knowing what's expected of him. He won't sit there wondering what to do, which dissolves self-confidence. He'll have an improved image and it will give him an edge."

8. Go Natural

Turn everyday situations into learning moments. For example, if someone in the supermarket smashes a cart, say, "I wonder what's going on with them?" If an ambulance roars by say "I hope everyone is okay." This could be more effective with younger children than bringing them to a soup kitchen. "Charity work is good, but be sensitive to your child's age. Strangers may produce anxiety," advises Szalavitz.

9. Be a Role Model

All of the experts agree: both parents should behave how they want to see their son behave. "This is easier said than done, but when kids see you donating to charity, being kind to other people or saying please and thank you, that has a big influence," says Szalavitz. "Children learn how to regulate themselves from their parents and caregivers." Remember to consider role models when selecting a nanny or other child care providers.

10. Work as a Team

It's important to create a plan and work together with your caregiver, so you are teaching the same skills. Pick a few lessons at a time and make sure everyone has the same age-appropriate steps in mind for your child. Review the tips above during your regular meetings and adjust them as your son grows.

Once your son gets into the routine of being a young gentleman, he will experience the benefits of being polite and acting kindly towards others. He'll soon see that it actually feels nice to be, well.... nice.

Eberle's ideas are an excellent starting point for parents of young children. Parents that struggle with defiant boys at a young age can be grateful that they have strong-willed boys who can be shaped and formed in their years of growth to become strong-willed gentlemen, something of which the world could always use a lot more of in numbers.

Even if you, as a parent, had a less-than-desirable upbringing, that's no reason not to have enough courage to raise your son to become a gentleman. In fact, it is often the pure and simple reason as to why a parent can and should find the courage within himself or herself to raise his or her son differently – to, in fact, raise his or her son to become a gentleman.

> *"We must develop and maintain the capacity to forgive. He who is devoid of the power to forgive is devoid of the power to love. There is some good in the worst of us and some evil in the best of us. When we discover this, we are less prone to hate our enemies."*
>
> *– Martin Luther King, Jr*

Additionally, if you're the parent of young children, and even if you're a parent of older children (because it's never too late to start working with your son to help him grow up to become a gentleman), you might start with a few simple rules, such as those I've listed below.

1) Start Young

This isn't to say that an older child, or even a teen or adult male, can't learn what it takes to be a gentleman. Although it can't be forced by any means, any boy or man can become a gentleman if that's what he wishes to become. However, the teaching is ingrained into the child's lifestyle when being a gentleman is taught from the time the child is old enough to understand speech and put words together to form sentences. Parents and caregivers that make a conscious effort to raise the boy to become a gentleman tend to succeed at it. When a boy is taught gentlemanly nature from the time he's very young, it becomes a part of his lifestyle. When being a gentleman is the goal of the parents and/or caregivers, a gentleman isn't something that he becomes. In other words, it is instead something that he is. With an older child or a teen, obviously the concept of starting young isn't possible, but that's no reason to give up before getting started.

2) Be Consistent

A true gentleman consistently lives by his values and holds his morals to a high standard, never wavering from his integrity or what he believes to be a proper gentleman.

3) Lead by Example

By living consistently to your own standards as a gentleman, those around you may start emulating your behavior due to your self-respect, as well as by observing how others treat and respect you. This is important for children, too, as they learn via the adults and older men around them. If you are successful, well respected and a gentleman, others will want that respect and success themselves, possibly aiding in the positive change of their own behavior in order to achieve it.

4) Don't Give Up

Change doesn't happen overnight, and there are endless ways gentlemanly behavior will pay off, earn respect and, ultimately, happiness. People will respect you, want to be around you, look up to you, and so forth. It takes time to change personal behaviors that don't serve you or those around you, so be patient with your growth and have faith that, with time, guidance and practice, you can become the true gentleman that you know you are capable of becoming.

*"You cannot be anything you want to be
– but you can be a lot more of who you already are."*

– Tom Rath

Photo Credit: Quinn Slocum

Being a Gentleman is Being Your Best You
Josua Slocum

Anyone who has had the gift of being in his presence will attest to the fact that my son, Jos Slocum, is the epitome of a Gentleman. He has all the general characteristics, like holding the door open or thinking of others first. But it is beyond graceful manners. What truly stands out is his heart and the kind way he treats everyone.

He has a positive outlook towards people in general. He has the best hopes for others right off the bat.

A Tribute to Grandpa Dody for Shaping His Life

This is a quality that he attributes to learning from his Grandpa Dody, who Jos says was a major influence in his life and development. "He never said anything bad about anyone." He was true to his word and worked hard. He had a really kind heart. What really made a mark was his Grandpa Dody's work ethic and the way he interacted with people. His undivided attention was with you. If Jos was doing something with his Grandpa, he was the only thing that was going on. He was like that with everybody. He would hold the door open for someone. That's what he was doing at that moment for that person. And they could feel it. And for him, it wasn't a chore; it was his pleasure.

Today's Culture of Empathy

When it comes to gentlemen in **today's society and culture,** Jos feels the world has evolved to empathetic men. But culture often confuses it with weakness, that being empathetic is being weak. For Jos, it's being so understanding and grateful for who you are and the things that you do on a consistent basis. It's an active practice to look for comparisons and ways to help other people. He is very grateful for what he has every day.

Being empathetic towards people and being a gentleman is not difficult. It's intentional versus passive empathy and has nothing to do with being a pushover. He feels the culture confuses it. Rather, it's taking the time to understand. Knowing that little things can really make a difference to anybody, even if they're just strangers.

Jos encourages you to take pride in the way you interact with everybody, not just the people you think matter. Make sure in one way or another, you make their lives a little bit better, even if it's a smile or a kind act. Help people feel important, like being gentle with your approach and doing those little acts consistently.

The Hero's Journey

Perhaps the embodiment of the concept of being a gentleman can be found in Joseph Campbell's **The Hero's Journey.** For Jos, reflecting on the things that he's done in his life and the experiences that he's had, it's the little hero's journeys that he identified in his life that have helped him go on the path to becoming even more of a gentleman. It's important to realize for most people that sometimes there's that thing that calls you to action. That thing that sets you out of your comfort zone and takes you to a new level of understanding of what it means to *you* to be a gentleman… in essence, *a better person.* According to the ultimate gentleman, Jos, *"A little self-reflection can do a lot of people good."*

Josua Slocum grew up traveling the world as I supported world renowned peak performance coach, Tony Robbins. Following his path, he graduated from the Gemological Institute of America, Class of 2017. He is a Customer Success Manager at Worthy.com and helps his clients gain clarity and simplifies the complex world of the jewelry resell market. Josua specializes in watches, diamond jewelry and a broad range of gemstones. He is also a Qualifying National Marketing Director with Juice Plus. A philanthropist from a very young age, Josua served as Chairman of St. Jude's Youth Board, Las Vegas Chapter in addition to participating in numerous Basket Brigades and other endeavors to contribute to communities all over the world.

Thank you for picking up this book. It was meant to be short, sweet and to the point. If we make these simple principles foundational for our boys, I TRULY believe that the future generations will benefit and set a new standard of what it means to Be the Change we wish to see in the world.

Being a gentleman is fairly simple…

It is doing the right thing every day of your life. To raise a gentleman, YOU have to do what you want your boys to grow up to be, you can't "blame" it on the school system, technology, or this current generation. It is our responsibility to have more awareness, to catch our boys doing things right and to acknowledge them when they do, and to *keep* acknowledging them, ALWAYS.

May our moral compass always guide us. It will take a lot of courage, faith and some people challenging you but it is worth it.

A percentage of all book sales will be donated to
organizations supporting our young gentlemen.

Additional Resources

Five Books for Boys on Their Way to Being a Gentleman

1. *Emily Post's Table Manners for Kids* by Peggy Post and Cindy Post Senning, Ed.D. Great nuts and bolts lessons on table manners and refresher course for grown-ups.

2. *What Do You Say, Dear?* by Sesyle Joslin and Maurice Sendak. Hilarious lessons on proper etiquette.

3. *The Berenstain Bears Say Please and Thank You* by Jan and Mike Berenstain. Classic book for understanding basic manners and getting along with others.

4. *Not Me!* by Nicola Killen. Adorable and beautifully illustrated story for teaching responsibility.

5. *Leonardo, the Terrible Monster* by Mo Willems. Creative, silly picture book about a boy learning empathy.

Works Cited

Brooks, Jacqueline Grennon, and Martin G. Brooks. In Search of Understanding: The Case for Constructivist Classrooms. Alexandria, VA: Association for Supervision and Curriculum Development, 1999. Print.

Eberle, Sara. "10 Tips to Raising a Gentleman." Care. Care.com, n.d. Web. 01 Nov. 2015. <https://www.care.com/a/10-tips-to-raising-a-gentleman-1205290905>.

Keeley, Arthur. "Raising a Gentleman." Focus on the Family Feb.-Mar. 2009: n. pag. Web. 1 Nov. 2015. <http://www.focusonthefamily.com/parenting/single-parents/building-a-strong-family/raising-a-gentleman>.

LaRuina, Richard. "How To Be A Gentleman: Why It's More Important Than Ever To Be The Modern Gentleman (Hint: Women Love It)." PUA Training. PUA Training, 29 Jan. 2013. Web. 4 Nov. 2015. <http://www.puatraining.com/blog/how-to-be-a-gentleman>.

"Life Isn't Promised So Get Busy Living." Web log post. Get Busy Living. Epic Living, Web. 6 Nov. 2015. <http://getbusylivingblog.com/life-is-not-promised-so-get-busy-living/>.

McNally, David. Even Eagles Need a Push: Learning to Soar in a Changing World. New York: Dell, 1990. Print.

Rath, Tom. Strengths Finder 2.0. New York: Gallup, 2007. Print.

Rath, Tom, and Barry Conchie. Strengths Based Leadership: Great Leaders, Teams, and Why People Follow. New York: Gallup, 2008. Print.

Ruiz, Don Miguel. The Four Agreements. San Rafael, CA: Amber-Allen, 1997. Print.

Praise & Reviews

"If you want to be an incredible parent and raise your sons to be powerful men built to serve and contribute, this is the blueprint.

It's a How-To guide on bringing back respect, chivalry and trust.

Loren crushes it and beautifully expresses step by step how to bring respect, honor and compassion back into our society and back into our homes.

This is a MUST-READ for any adult who so wants to reconnect with their children and raise them as kind and compassionate future leaders."

– Setema Gali Jr., High Performance Coach

"The first time I met Loren we were sharing the stage at an event. Besides her huge presence and her beauty , her energy and humor light up the room. When she talked about her boys, I knew they were gentlemen. As a mother of 3 boys , I am so excited for everyone to embrace the simple truths in this book. She became a role model for me and my boys.

– Stefania Lo Gatto

"Loren Lahav is one of my favorite people and has been a game changer in my life. Her generous spirit, her brilliant mind, her ability to get things done, relate to anyone, and her ability to connect people at a very high level. I have met some incredible entrepreneurs and global influencers through her. She always knows the right person to connect with. I've had the privilege to work with Loren both front stage and backstage. Witnessing her move an audience of 9,000 people through her story telling and authentic 'Stay True' approach is fascinating to watch. In fact, I put her in the top 5 speakers I've ever seen. Loren is someone who simply gets it. From working with successful CEO's and entrepreneurs to serving impoverished people around the world, she is a true servant leader and a big difference maker. An incredible mother, executive, speaker, author, creator and friend. I'm glad I have her in my inner circle.

I can think of no one better to author a book called, 'The Courage to Raise a Gentleman' than Loren Lahav. She walks the walk by being a loving mother who will do anything for her kids and someone who is out in the world living life on her terms. Her sons are brilliant young men who she raised to be perfect gentlemen and though her example is helping other have the courage to raise gentlemen as well. Loren is the exact kind of woman you want to model if you want to raise your sons to be gentlemen... not because she has ALL of the answers, but because she knows all of the people who do!"

– Kevin Donahue

"The Courage to Raise a Gentleman" is one of the timeliest pieces of work to hit the market in decades. We live in a time of complete confusion for Men and our boys. Who better to write this guide than Loren Lahav? A mother who is not just pontificating a theoretical opinion, but rather recording for us the steps she took to actually raise 2 gentlemen who are now serving and making a mark on this planet for good!! I personally wish I would have had this book for my parents! Most do what they know, and what they know is sometimes a generational curse of well-meaning but harmful parenting. I had to learn as an adult how to be a gentleman from great men and specifically from this woman. She challenged me to become a better man, to live up to a potential she saw. She is my hero and more importantly a hero to the boys who know her best and that have now grown into stellar young men. I highly suggest you buy this blueprint to guiding our future men to engage in this world as strong, loving gentlemen rather than retreating and hiding from the call to lead. Buy it. Buy it and live it now!!!"

– Jason Sisneros, aka "The Bald Avenger"

"Written from the experience and heart of a mother, wife and personal growth teacher, The Courage to Raise a Gentleman fills a growing need in our society: more good men. Loren gives many take-home tools to raise men rooted in empathy. One day a grandmother told me: 'My new daughter-in-law gave me the supreme compliment: thank you for raising such a sensitive man.' Wow! Another must-read and must-do feature of this book is the importance of quality mentors. Growing up as a child of a single mom, my wise mother surrounded me with wise male mentors that became empathy influencers in my life. Thanks, Mom! A male-modelling lesson I tell my sons and new fathers: 'Be the man you want your daughter to marry.' This book will show you how. I highly recommend it."

– William Sears, MD. Author: *The Dr. Sears T5 Wellness Plan, makeover your mind and body, 5 changes in 5 weeks*

"Loren Lahav brings her understanding, compassion and fiery humor into your life. Her heartfelt words keep you on a path of gratitude, while inspiring growth and awareness in your day to day life."

– Jeni Hott, Founder of Global Bloggers United and mom of a 4-year-old gentleman

About Loren Lahav

North Carolina native Loren Lahav grew up watching her "gentleman" father in action and learning not only how to behave in the world, but how to pass those lessons onto her own family. Today, she is a mother, author, international speaker, life coach, and business coach who is renowned for the value she brings to every endeavor.

She is a real estate investor and one of her businesses has teams in 25 countries. She frequently speaks to large audiences, sharing the stage with some of the world's most influential leaders while addressing influential companies including Lululemon, Zappos, Hilton Hotels, Four Seasons Hotels, LifeAid, just to name a few. Loren has been featured in media such as People Magazine, Success Magazine, Ladies Home Journal, Woman's Day, Fox News' "The Strategy Room," and Oprah Radio. She has also created her own signature projects—Badass and Beautiful, Unapologetically Authentic, and the True Health Cleanse—which guide clients through both internal and external transformations.

Creator of the I AM Card Series and I AM Planner, she is also The author of *Life Tuneups, The Greatest Love, The Divorce Detox* and Co-Author of *Chicken Soup for the Soul: Time to Thrive,* Loren's most recent book is *The Courage to Raise a Gentleman: Building an Extraordinary Foundation for Self, Family and Humanity.*

www.ingramcontent.com/pod-product-compliance
Lightning Source LLC
Chambersburg PA
CBHW060806110426
42739CB00032BA/3113